Recipes: American Cooking

Contents

Foods of the World

TIME-LIFE BOOKS, NEW YORK

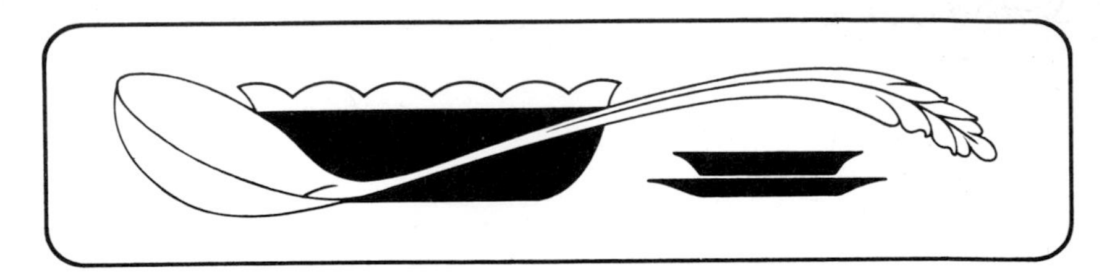

New England Clam Chowder

To serve 6 to 8

- 1/4 pound salt pork, cut into 1/8-inch dice
- 1 cup finely chopped onion
- 3 cups cold water
- 4 cups potatoes, cut into 1/4-inch dice
- 2 dozen shucked hard-shelled clams with their juice, coarsely chopped, or two 8-ounce cans chopped clams (about 2 cups)
- 2 cups heavy or light cream
- 1/8 teaspoon thyme
- Salt
- Freshly ground black pepper
- 2 tablespoons soft butter
- Paprika

Over high heat, fry the diced salt pork in a heavy 2-quart saucepan, stirring constantly for about 3 minutes until a thin film of fat covers the bottom of the pan. Reduce the heat to moderate, stir in the chopped onion and cook together for about 5 minutes longer, stirring occasionally. When the diced pork and onions turn a light golden brown, add 3 cups of water and the diced potatoes. Bring to a boil over high heat, then reduce the heat and simmer with the pan half covered for about 15 minutes until the potatoes are tender but not falling apart.

Add the chopped clams and their juices, the cream and thyme, and heat almost to the boiling point. Then taste and season with as much salt and pepper as you think it needs. Stir in the soft butter. Serve the chowder in large individual bowls with each portion dusted with a little paprika. Pilot crackers are the traditional accompaniment.

Seafood Gumbo

To serve 8 to 10

8 tablespoons butter
2 ten-ounce packages of frozen okra, thoroughly defrosted and thinly sliced, or 1 pound fresh okra, thinly sliced
½ cup finely chopped onion
½ cup finely chopped green pepper
½ teaspoon finely chopped garlic
2 tablespoons flour
4 cups chicken stock, fresh or canned
2 cups coarsely chopped fresh ripe tomatoes, or an equivalent amount of drained canned tomatoes
Herb bouquet of 6 sprigs parsley and a large bay leaf, tied with cord
½ teaspoon thyme
2 teaspoons salt
Freshly ground black pepper
1 pound of small raw shrimp, shelled and deveined
½ pound of lump crab meat, fresh or canned
16 oysters, shucked
2 teaspoons lemon juice
2 teaspoons Worcestershire sauce
¼ teaspoon Tabasco
2 cups hot steamed rice (optional)

In a 10- to 12-inch frying pan, melt 4 tablespoons of the butter over moderate heat. Add the fresh or frozen okra and, stirring constantly, cook until the okra stops "roping," that is, until the white threads the vegetable produces disappear. Over moderate heat, melt the remaining 4 tablespoons of butter in a heavy 2- or 3-quart soup pot or casserole. When the foam subsides, add the onion, green pepper and garlic, and cook without browning for about 5 minutes. Stir in the 2 tablespoons of flour, and when it has been absorbed by the vegetables, cook 2 to 3 minutes longer, stirring constantly. Pour in the chicken stock and stir with a whisk to dissolve the flour. Then add the okra, the tomatoes, the herb bouquet, thyme, salt and a few grindings of black pepper. Bring to a boil, turn the heat to its lowest point and simmer, partially covered, for ½ hour. Then drop in the shrimp, simmer for 5 minutes and add the crab meat and oysters. Simmer for 2 or 3 minutes, or only until the oysters curl around the edges and the crab meat is heated through. Season with the lemon juice, Worcestershire sauce and the ¼ teaspoon Tabasco, or more to taste.

To serve, it is customary to ladle the gumbo over small mounds of hot rice in deep soup plates. However, the rice may be omitted if you prefer.

Crawfish Bisque with Stuffed Heads

To serve 8 to 10

5 pounds live crawfish
4 quarts water
2 cups coarsely chopped onion
Herb bouquet of 3 sprigs parsley, 1 bay leaf, 1/4 teaspoon thyme, 6 peppercorns tied together in cheesecloth
8 tablespoons butter
1 cup finely chopped onion
1/2 cup finely diced carrot
1/2 cup finely diced celery
1 teaspoon finely chopped garlic
2 tablespoons finely chopped parsley
3/4 teaspoon thyme
8 tablespoons flour
2 teaspoons salt
2 tablespoons paprika

Wash the crawfish under cold running water, then soak in water for at least 10 minutes. In a heavy 8- to 10-quart pot, bring 4 quarts of water to a rapid boil. Add the chopped onion and the herb bouquet. Then drop in all the crawfish a handful at a time and boil uncovered for about 5 minutes. Remove the crawfish and set aside. Strain the cooking liquid through cheesecloth, then return it to the thoroughly washed pot.

In a heavy skillet, melt the butter over moderate heat. When the foam subsides, add the onion, carrot, celery, garlic, parsley and thyme. Cook for about 5 minutes, until the vegetables are limp but not brown, then stir in the flour. Stir this mixture over low heat for about 10 minutes. With a rubber spatula, scrape it into the crawfish stock. Bring to a boil, mixing with a whisk until the stock thickens slightly. Turn the heat to low and simmer gently while you shell the crawfish.

Break the heads from the crawfish and pick the meat from the tails, adding the tail shells to the simmering stock as you proceed. Discard the vein in the tail meat, chop the meat fine and reserve in a bowl. In another bowl, shake the yellow fat from the crawfish heads by gently tapping them against the sides of the bowl. With a small knife, scrape the heads clean of any black matter and set aside 35 to 40 of them to be stuffed. Add the remaining heads to the stock, and stir in the 2 teaspoons of salt and the paprika. Simmer partially covered for 45 minutes.

STUFFING (for about 40 heads)
2 tablespoons butter
3 tablespoons minced onion
1/2 teaspoon finely chopped garlic
1 1/2 cups fresh bread crumbs
1 egg yolk, lightly beaten
3 tablespoons chopped parsley
2 tablespoons sherry
1/2 teaspoon salt
Pinch of cayenne

While the bisque is simmering, make the stuffing. In a small skillet, melt 2 tablespoons of butter over moderate heat. When the foam subsides, add the minced onion and garlic and cook for about 4 minutes, or until they are transparent but not brown. Scrape them into a mixing bowl. Add half the reserved crawfish meat, the bread crumbs, egg yolk, parsley, sherry, salt and cayenne, mix and taste for seasoning. Pack each head with stuffing, then place in one layer in a shallow baking dish. Dot with soft butter and bake for about 10 minutes in a preheated 350° oven.

Before serving, strain the bisque through a fine sieve and discard the crawfish shells. Bring the bisque to a simmer once more, and add the remaining crawfish meat. Divide the stuffed heads among individual soup plates, pour the hot bisque over them and serve.

Cheddar Cheese Soup

To serve 6 to 8

2 tablespoons butter
¼ cup finely chopped onion
¼ cup finely chopped carrot
¼ cup finely chopped green pepper
¼ cup finely chopped celery
3 tablespoons flour
5 cups chicken stock, fresh or canned
½ pound Cheddar cheese, coarsely grated (about 2 cups)
1½ cups milk
Salt
White pepper

In a 2- to 3-quart saucepan melt the butter over moderate heat. When the foam subsides add the onion, carrot, green pepper and the celery, and cook for 6 to 8 minutes or until the vegetables are soft but not brown. Mix in the flour and pour in the stock. Bring to a boil over moderate heat, beating constantly with a whisk until it thickens slightly. Then reduce the heat to low and simmer the soup, partially covered, for about 10 minutes, stirring occasionally. Now, a handful at a time, beat in the cheese and cook until it dissolves, then pour in 1 cup of the milk, adding up to ½ cup more if the soup is too thick. It should have the consistency of heavy cream. Bring almost to a boil, then strain through a fine sieve into another saucepan. Taste for seasoning, and add as much salt and white pepper as you think is needed. Heat once more almost to the boiling point and serve. Cheddar soup is equally good cold. Chill it thoroughly and serve it in chilled cups or soup plates.

Cold Split Pea Soup with Mint

To serve 6 to 8

2 cups dry green split peas
2 quarts chicken stock, fresh or canned
1 cup coarsely chopped onion
1 stalk celery, coarsely chopped
1/8 teaspoon ground cloves
1 bay leaf
1 cup coarsely chopped fresh mint
1 teaspoon salt
Pinch white pepper
1/2 to 1 cup chilled heavy cream
Sprigs of fresh mint

Wash the split peas thoroughly under cold running water and continue to wash until the draining water runs clear. Pick over the peas and discard any discolored ones. In a heavy 4- to 5-quart saucepan or soup kettle, bring the chicken stock to a boil and drop in the peas slowly so that the stock does not stop boiling. Add the onions, celery, cloves, bay leaf and mint. Reduce the heat and simmer with the pan partially covered for 1 1/2 hours or until the peas can be easily mashed with a spoon. Remove the bay leaf.

Purée the soup through a food mill or fine sieve into a large bowl, and then rub it through the sieve back into the saucepan or into another bowl. Add the salt and pepper, and chill the soup in the refrigerator. (If you wish to serve the soup immediately, place the soup in a bowl and set the bowl in a larger container filled with crushed ice or ice cubes. With a metal spoon, stir the soup until it is ice cold.) Before serving, stir in 1/2 to 1 cup of chilled heavy cream, thinning the soup as desired, and taste for seasoning. Garnish with sprigs of fresh mint.

Black Bean Soup

To serve 6 to 8

- 1 pound black turtle beans (2 cups)
- 1 cup coarsely chopped onion
- 1 cup coarsely chopped celery with leaves
- 1 bay leaf
- 3 smoked ham hocks
- 10 cups water
- ½ to 1 cup water or chicken stock, fresh or canned (optional)
- Salt
- Freshly ground black pepper
- 4 hard-cooked eggs, coarsely chopped
- 2 tablespoons red-wine vinegar
- Lemon slices
- Parsley sprigs

Wash the beans in a sieve under cold running water. When the water runs clear, transfer the beans to a large soup pot. Add the onion, celery, bay leaf and ham hocks. Pour in the 10 cups of water and bring to a boil over high heat. Skim off any scum that rises to the surface, half cover the pot and reduce the heat to low. Simmer the soup for 2½ to 3 hours, or until the beans are soft enough to be crushed easily with a fork. Remove the ham hocks and the bay leaf, and purée the soup through a food mill or sieve. Do not use an electric blender. Return the purée and all its liquid to the soup pot. If it seems too thick, thin it with as much chicken stock or water as you think it needs. Taste for seasoning, and add salt and a few grindings of black pepper. Bring the soup to a simmer. Just before serving, stir in the hard-cooked eggs and the vinegar. Garnish each portion with a slice of lemon topped with a small sprig of parsley.

Cucumber Bisque

To serve 4

6 tablespoons butter
2 medium onions, finely chopped (1 cup)
2 large cucumbers, peeled and finely chopped (2 cups)
3 cups chicken stock, fresh or canned
2 tablespoons flour
2 egg yolks
1/2 cup heavy cream
1 medium-sized cucumber, peeled and diced into 1/4-inch pieces
Salt
White pepper
2 tablespoons finely chopped fresh parsley or chives

In a heavy 2- to 3-quart saucepan, melt 4 tablespoons of the butter over moderate heat. When the foam subsides, stir in the chopped onions and the chopped cucumbers and, stirring occasionally, cook them for about 5 minutes until the onions are transparent but not brown.

Add the chicken stock and bring to a boil. Lower the heat and simmer, uncovered, for 20 to 30 minutes, or until the vegetables are tender. Pour the soup into a sieve set over a large bowl and force the vegetables through with the back of a wooden spoon.

Melt the remaining 2 tablespoons of butter in the saucepan. Remove the pan from the heat and stir in the flour. Pour in the puréed soup, beating vigorously with a wire whisk. Return to moderate heat and cook about 3 to 5 minutes, whisking constantly, until the soup has thickened slightly.

In a small bowl, combine the egg yolks and heavy cream. Beating constantly with a whisk, pour into it 1 cup of the hot soup, 2 tablespoons at a time. Then reverse the process. Slowly pour this warmed mixture back into the remaining soup, still beating with the whisk. Simmer over very low heat for 5 minutes but do not let the soup come to a boil. Just before serving, stir in the diced raw cucumber, season with salt and white pepper, and sprinkle with the chopped parsley or chives.

To serve the soup cold, let it cool to room temperature, then cover and refrigerate for at least 3 hours. Add the diced raw cucumbers, seasonings and chopped herbs just before serving. If you like, you may serve the cold soup with a spoonful of slightly salted, stiffly whipped cream in each portion, or a spoonful of sour cream may be used.

Pumpkin Soup

To serve 4 to 6

1 tablespoon butter
2 tablespoons finely chopped onion
2 cups cooked pumpkin, canned or fresh, thoroughly drained
2½ cups chicken stock, fresh or canned
2½ cups milk
⅛ teaspoon ground cloves
½ teaspoon sugar
1 teaspoon lemon juice
2 to 3 drops Tabasco
½ teaspoon salt
¼ cup heavy cream

In a heavy 4-quart saucepan, melt the butter over moderate heat. When the foam subsides, add the onions and cook for 2 or 3 minutes, stirring, until they are transparent but not brown. Add the pumpkin, chicken stock, milk, the cloves, sugar, lemon juice, Tabasco and salt. Stir thoroughly to blend all the ingredients.

Bring to a boil, then reduce the heat to its lowest point and cook the soup, stirring occasionally, for 15 minutes. Then purée the soup by forcing it through a fine sieve or food mill into a large mixing bowl. Do not use a blender; it will result in too bland and smooth a texture. Stir in the cream. Return the soup to the saucepan and heat it through without letting it come to a boil. Taste for seasoning, garnish with croutons, if desired, and serve hot.

NOTE: This pumpkin soup may also be served chilled. If you serve the soup cold, omit the croutons and garnish each serving with a thin slice of peeled, chilled orange.

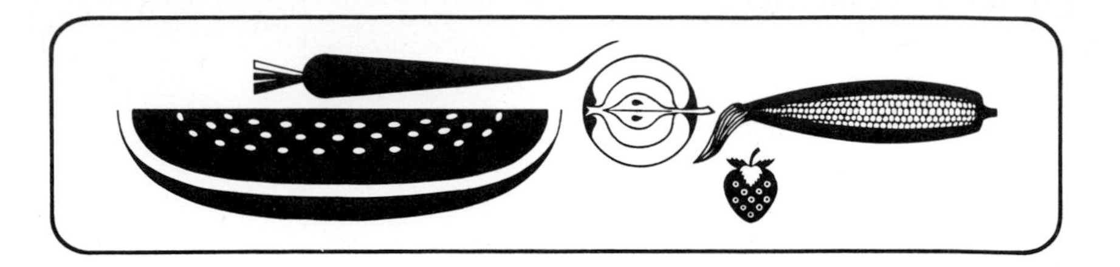

Pennsylvania Dutch Fried Tomatoes

To serve 4 to 6

4 to 5 large firm ripe tomatoes, 3 to 4 inches in diameter, thickly sliced
2 teaspoons salt
Freshly ground black pepper
½ cup flour
4 to 6 tablespoons butter
2 tablespoons sieved brown sugar
1 cup heavy cream
1 tablespoon finely chopped fresh parsley

Sprinkle the tomatoes on both sides with salt and a few grindings of black pepper. Then dip the tomato slices in the flour, coating each side thoroughly and very gently shaking off any excess. In a 12-inch heavy skillet, preferably of the nonstick variety, melt the butter over moderate heat.

When the foam subsides, add the tomato slices and cook them for about 5 minutes, or until they are lightly browned. Sprinkle the tops with half the brown sugar, carefully turn the tomatoes over with a spatula and sprinkle with the rest of the brown sugar. Cook for 3 to 4 minutes, then transfer the slices to a heated serving platter.

Pour the cream into the pan, raise the heat to high and bring the cream to a boil, stirring constantly. Boil briskly for 2 to 3 minutes, or until the cream thickens. Taste for seasoning, then pour over the tomatoes. Sprinkle with the finely chopped parsley.

NOTE: Traditionally, this recipe is made with green tomatoes; however, they are not easily available. If you can find them, cook them somewhat more slowly and for a few minutes longer on each side.

Creamed Onions and Peas

To serve 8

24 to 28 peeled white onions, about 1 inch in diameter
3 cups fresh green peas (about 2 pounds), or 3 packages frozen green peas, thoroughly defrosted
4 tablespoons butter
4 tablespoons flour
1½ cups milk
½ cup cream
1 teaspoon salt
Pinch of white pepper
¼ teaspoon nutmeg

Place the onions in a 3- or 4-quart saucepan with enough water to cover them by about an inch. Salt the water lightly. Bring to a boil, then reduce the heat to its lowest point and simmer the onions partially covered for about 20 minutes, or until they show only the slightest resistance when pierced with the tip of a small, sharp knife. Drain the onions in a sieve set over a small bowl and set aside. Reserve the cooking water to use in making the sauce.

Cook the fresh peas by dropping them into 6 or 7 quarts of rapidly boiling salted water. Boil them briskly uncovered for 8 to 10 minutes, or until they are tender. Then drain the peas and immerse them in a bowl of cold water for 2 or 3 minutes. This will stop their cooking and help keep their bright green color. Drain again and put the peas aside with the cooked onions. Frozen peas need not be cooked, merely defrosted.

In a heavy 3-quart saucepan, melt the butter over moderate heat and stir in the flour. Remove the pan from the heat and pour in the 2 cups of the reserved onion-cooking liquid, beating with a wire whisk until the flour-butter mixture is partially dissolved. Add the milk and cream, return the pan to the heat and cook, whisking constantly, until the sauce is smooth and thick.

Simmer for 3 to 4 minutes to remove any taste of uncooked flour, season with the salt, white pepper and nutmeg, then add the cooked onions and the cooked fresh peas or thoroughly defrosted frozen peas. Simmer for 5 minutes, or until the vegetables are heated through. Taste for seasoning and serve.

Spiced Acorn Squash

To serve 8

4 medium-sized acorn squash
1/2 cup dark brown sugar
1 teaspoon cinnamon
1/2 teaspoon grated nutmeg
1/4 teaspoon ground cloves
1/2 teaspoon salt
8 tablespoons melted butter (1 quarter-pound stick)
1/2 cup maple syrup
Eight 1/2-inch pieces of bacon
About 2 cups boiling water

Preheat the oven to 350°. Cut each squash in half and with a teaspoon scrape out the seeds and fibers. In a small bowl combine the brown sugar, cinnamon, nutmeg, cloves, salt and melted butter, and stir them together thoroughly.

Arrange the squash in a shallow ovenproof baking dish large enough to hold them all comfortably. Spoon an equal amount of the spiced butter mixture into the hollow of each squash and over that pour a teaspoon or so of maple syrup. Top with a piece of bacon. Now add boiling water to the baking dish—the water should be about 1 inch deep. Bake in the middle of the oven for 30 minutes, or until the squash can be easily pierced with the tip of a small, sharp knife. Serve at once.

Mushrooms and Onions in Sour Cream

To serve 4 to 6

4 tablespoons butter
2 medium onions, thinly sliced
1 pound fresh mushrooms, 1 to 1 1/2 inches in diameter
1 cup sour cream
1 teaspoon lemon juice
1 teaspoon salt
Freshly ground black pepper
2 teaspoons finely chopped fresh parsley

In a heavy 10-inch skillet, melt the butter over medium heat. When the foam subsides, add the onions and cook for 6 to 8 minutes until they are lightly colored. Stir in the mushrooms, cover the pan and cook, still over moderate heat, for about 7 minutes. Add the sour cream, lemon juice, salt and a few grindings of pepper; simmer, stirring, until the cream is heated through. Don't let it boil. Taste for seasoning and sprinkle with chopped parsley. Serve as a first course over pieces of freshly made buttered toast, as a vegetable to accompany a main dish, or as a luncheon or supper dish in the center of or around a molded spinach ring *(opposite)*.

Spinach Ring

To serve 4 to 6

2 tablespoons butter
2 tablespoons flour
1/2 cup milk
3 egg yolks
2 ten-ounce packages chopped frozen spinach, thoroughly defrosted and squeezed dry, or 1 1/4 pounds fresh spinach, cooked, drained, squeezed dry and finely chopped
1/2 teaspoon grated onion
3/4 teaspoon salt
1/8 teaspoon white pepper
3 egg whites

Preheat the oven to 350°. Lightly butter and flour a 1 1/2-quart ring mold. Melt the 2 tablespoons of butter in a heavy 3- or 4-quart saucepan, remove from heat and stir in the 2 tablespoons of flour. Then pour in the milk and stir with a whisk until the flour is partially dissolved. Return the pan to low heat, and cook, stirring constantly, until the sauce comes almost to a boil and is thick and smooth. Remove from heat and beat in the egg yolks, one at a time, whisking until each one is thoroughly blended in before adding the next. Stir in the spinach, grated onion, salt and pepper, and allow the mixture to cool slightly.

Beat the egg whites with a wire whisk or rotary beater—and in an unlined copper bowl if possible—until they are stiff enough to form unwavering peaks on the beater when it is lifted from the bowl. Stir a large spoonful of egg white into the spinach mixture and then gently fold in the remaining egg whites. Ladle the mixture into the mold. Place the mold in a baking pan and pour enough boiling water into the baking pan to reach 2/3 of the way up the sides of the mold. Bake on the middle shelf of the oven for 30 minutes, or until it is firm to the touch.

To turn out the spinach ring, wipe dry the outside of the mold and run a knife around its inside surfaces. Place a serving plate upside down over the top of the mold, and, firmly grasping plate and mold together, invert the two. Rap them sharply on a table, and the spinach ring should slide out easily onto the plate. Serve at once.

Cabbage in White Wine

To serve 6 to 8

- 8 tablespoons (1 quarter-pound stick) butter
- 3 pounds green cabbage, cored and coarsely chopped
- 1 cup dry white wine, such as a California Chablis
- 1 teaspoon fresh tarragon or ½ teaspoon dried
- 1 teaspoon salt
- Freshly ground black pepper

In a heavy 10- or 12-inch skillet, melt the butter over moderate heat. When the foam subsides, add the cabbage and, with a fork, toss it in the melted butter until it is well coated. Cook uncovered, stirring occasionally, for 10 minutes, then add the wine, tarragon, salt and a few grindings of pepper.

Bring to a boil, cover tightly and reduce the heat to low. Simmer for 5 to 10 minutes, or until the cabbage is tender. With a slotted spoon, remove the cabbage from the pan to a heated vegetable dish or platter. Boil the liquid in the pan rapidly, uncovered, for a few minutes to concentrate its flavor before pouring it over the cabbage.

Celery Victor

Celery Victor was named after Victor Hirtzler, the San Francisco chef who created it at the St. Francis Hotel.

To serve 6

- 3 bunches celery, about 2 inches in diameter
- 1½ cups chicken stock, fresh or canned
- An herb bouquet of 4 sprigs parsley, 1 bay leaf and celery leaves tied together
- Salt
- Freshly ground black pepper
- 3 tablespoons white-wine vinegar
- ½ cup olive oil
- 12 flat anchovy fillets
- 12 strips pimiento
- 6 slices tomato (optional)
- 6 slices hard-cooked eggs (optional)
- 1½ teaspoons finely chopped fresh parsley

Remove the outer stalks of the celery, leaving a heart about 1 inch wide and 6 inches long. Cut each celery heart in half lengthwise. Cut away all but the small leaves and trim the root ends (do not cut too deep; the celery halves should hold together). Use the cut-away leaves for the herb bouquet. With a sharp knife, scrape the outer stalks if they seem coarse.

Arrange the celery halves side by side in a 10- or 12-inch skillet, preferably enameled or stainless steel, and pour in the stock, using more stock or water if the celery is not completely covered. Add the herb bouquet, with as much salt and pepper as suits your taste, and bring to a boil. Reduce the heat to its lowest point, cover tightly and simmer the celery for about 15 minutes, or until it shows no resistance when pierced with the tip of a sharp knife. With tongs or a slotted spoon, transfer the celery halves to a deep platter that will hold them in a single layer.

With a whisk, beat the vinegar and the oil together and pour over the celery while it is still warm. Refrigerate for at least an hour before serving. To serve, arrange the celery halves on individual chilled plates and crisscross 2 anchovy fillets and 2 strips of pimiento over each serving. Or instead, if you prefer, garnish the celery with a slice of tomato and a slice of hard-cooked egg. In either case, moisten the celery with a spoonful or so of the vinegar-olive oil sauce and sprinkle with chopped parsley.

Wild Rice with Mushrooms

To serve 4 to 6

4 tablespoons butter
2 tablespoons finely diced scraped carrots
2 tablespoons finely diced celery
2 tablespoons finely chopped onion
1 cup wild rice
1 teaspoon salt
2 cups chicken stock, fresh or canned
1/2 pound mushrooms, coarsely chopped
2 tablespoons finely chopped fresh parsley
1/4 cup finely chopped pecans

In a heavy enameled or stainless-steel 2-quart saucepan, melt 2 tablespoons of the butter over moderate heat, and, when the foam subsides, add the carrots, celery and onions, cover and cook for 10 to 15 minutes, stirring occasionally, until the vegetables are soft but not brown. Stir in the cup of rice and the salt and cook for 2 to 3 minutes uncovered, stirring to coat the rice thoroughly with the butter. In a small saucepan bring the stock to a boil and pour it over the rice. Bring to a boil again, cover tightly and reduce the heat to its lowest point. Cook undisturbed for 25 to 30 minutes, or until the rice is tender and has absorbed all the stock.

Meanwhile, over moderate heat melt the remaining 2 tablespoons of butter in an enameled or stainless-steel skillet. When the foam subsides, add the mushrooms and parsley; cook, stirring, for 5 minutes. Add the pecans and cook for 2 to 3 minutes more. With a fork, stir the contents of the skillet into the finished rice. Taste for seasoning and serve.

Buttermilk Fried Onions

To serve 4 to 6

3 egg yolks
1½ cups flour
½ teaspoon baking soda
1½ teaspoons salt
2 cups buttermilk
Vegetable oil or shortening for deep frying
4 large yellow onions, 3 to 4 inches in diameter, peeled and cut in ¼-inch-thick slices
Salt

In a mixing bowl, combine the egg yolks, flour, baking soda and salt, and beat them together with a large spoon. Pour in the buttermilk slowly, beating until the mixture forms a fairly smooth paste. Heat the shortening in a deep-fat fryer—the fat should be at least 3 inches deep—until it registers 375° on a deep-fat thermometer.

Separate the onion slices into rings, drop them in the batter and then, 7 or 8 rings at a time, fry them in the fat for 4 to 5 minutes until lightly browned. Transfer them to paper towels while you proceed with the next batch. When all the onion rings are done, fry them again in the hot fat for a minute or two to heat them through and crisp them. Drain on paper towels and serve sprinkled with salt.

Corn Oysters

To make about 20

1 cup grated fresh corn (from 3 to 4 medium-sized cobs)
1 egg yolk, beaten
2 tablespoons flour
¼ teaspoon salt
Freshly ground black pepper
1 egg white
¼ to ½ cup vegetable shortening
Salt

In a small mixing bowl, combine the grated corn, egg yolk, flour, salt and a few grindings of black pepper. With a whisk or rotary beater, beat the egg white until it forms unwavering peaks on the beater when it is lifted out of the bowl. Gently but thoroughly fold it into the corn mixture.

In an 8- to 10-inch heavy skillet, heat 2 tablespoons of shortening over high heat until a light haze forms over it. Drop the batter by teaspoonfuls into the fat (the corn oysters should be about the size of silver dollars) and fry them for a minute or two on each side, watching them carefully for any sign of burning and regulating the heat accordingly. Drain the corn oysters on paper towels, batch by batch as you proceed, and add more shortening to the pan as needed. There should be a thin film of fat on the bottom of the pan at all times. Before serving on a heated platter, sprinkle the corn oysters liberally with salt. These make good accompaniments to meat and chicken dishes.

Boston Baked Beans

To serve 6 to 8

- 4 cups dried pea or Great Northern beans
- 3 medium-sized whole onions, peeled
- 2 teaspoons salt
- 4 cloves
- ½ cup molasses
- 1 cup brown sugar
- 2 teaspoons dry mustard
- 1 teaspoon black pepper
- 2 cups water
- ½ pound salt pork, scored

Put the beans in a large saucepan and pour in enough cold water to cover them by at least 2 inches. Bring to a boil, let boil for 2 minutes, then let the beans soak in the water off the heat for about 1 hour. Bring them to a boil again, add 1 onion and 1 teaspoon of the salt, half cover the pan and simmer the beans as slowly as possible for about 30 minutes, or until they are partially done. Drain the beans and discard the onion and bean water.

Preheat the oven to 250°. To bake the beans, choose a traditional 2½-quart bean pot or a heavy casserole with a tight-fitting cover. Place 2 onions, each stuck with 2 cloves, in the bottom of the bean pot or casserole and cover with the beans. In a small mixing bowl, combine the molasses, ¾ cup of the brown sugar, mustard, and 1 teaspoon each of salt and black pepper. Slowly stirring with a large spoon, pour in the 2 cups of water.

Pour this mixture over the beans and push the salt pork slightly beneath the surface. Cover tightly and bake in the center of the oven for 4½ to 5 hours. Then remove the cover and sprinkle with the remaining ¼ cup of brown sugar. Bake the beans uncovered for another ½ hour and serve.

Hashed Brown Potatoes

To serve 4 to 6

6 medium-sized boiling potatoes (about 2 pounds), peeled and cut into quarters

1/4 pound sliced bacon
2 tablespoons butter
1 teaspoon salt
Freshly ground black pepper

Bring 2 quarts of lightly salted water to a boil in a 4- to 5-quart pot and boil the potatoes uncovered until they can be easily pierced with the tip of a small, sharp knife. Drain the potatoes in a colander, return to the pan in which they were cooked or put them in a large, dry skillet and shake over moderate heat until they are dry.

Let the potatoes cool, then cut them into small dice. In a heavy 10- to 12-inch skillet, preferably one with a good nonstick surface, cook the bacon until it has rendered all of its fat and is crisp and brown. Remove the bacon with a slotted spoon and drain on paper towels. Add the butter to the bacon fat and place over moderate heat until the butter melts. Add the potatoes, and sprinkle them with the salt and a few grindings of black pepper. Then press the potatoes down firmly into the pan with a spatula. Cook over moderate heat, shaking the pan occasionally to prevent the potatoes from sticking. A brown crust should form on the bottom surface of the potatoes in about 20 minutes. Check by gently lifting the edge of the potatoes with a spatula. Cook a few minutes longer, raising the heat if necessary to achieve the proper color. They should be golden brown and crusty. To serve, cover the skillet with a heated platter and, grasping skillet and plate together, turn them upside down. The potatoes should fall out easily. Serve at once, sprinkled with the crumbled reserved bacon if desired.

Mashed Potatoes

To serve 8

4 quarts water
1 tablespoon salt
4 pounds baking potatoes
½ pound butter, softened
½ to 1 cup cream, preferably heavy
1 teaspoon salt
½ teaspoon white pepper
2 to 4 tablespoons melted butter (optional)
1 tablespoon finely chopped parsley, chives or dill (optional)

Bring the 4 quarts of water to a boil in a 6- to 8-quart pot. Add 1 tablespoon of salt. Meanwhile peel the potatoes, cut them into halves or quarters and drop them into the boiling water. Boil them briskly, uncovered, until they are tender. Test for doneness by piercing them periodically with the tip of a small, sharp knife. They should show no resistance in the center, but they should not fall apart. Drain them at once in a colander.

Return the potatoes to the pan in which they cooked, or transfer them to a large, heavy skillet and shake them over moderate heat for 2 to 3 minutes until they are as dry as possible. Then purée them into a heated mixing bowl either by mashing them with a potato masher, or by forcing through a potato ricer or through a large, coarse sieve with the back of a spoon.

Now, 2 or 3 tablespoons at a time, beat into the purée, either by hand or with an electric mixer, the ½ pound of softened butter. Heat the cream in a small saucepan and beat it into the potatoes a few tablespoons at a time, using as much as you need to give the purée the consistency that you prefer.

Ideally the mashed potatoes should be neither too wet nor too dry, and they should hold their shape lightly in a spoon. Beat in the salt and the white pepper, and taste for seasoning. Add more salt if you think it is necessary. Serve at once in a heated vegetable dish. If you like, float the melted butter in a well in the center of the potatoes and sprinkle them with one of the herbs.

Potato Salad

To make 2 quarts

3 pounds new potatoes, unpeeled
1 teaspoon salt
2 tablespoons white-wine vinegar
3/4 cup finely chopped celery
3/4 cup finely chopped onion
1 1/2 cups finely chopped green pepper
2 tablespoons finely chopped fresh parsley

Place the potatoes in boiling salted water to cover, and cook until they are tender but do not fall apart when gently pierced with a knife. Drain them in a colander and when they are cool enough to handle, peel and cut them into 1/2- to 3/4-inch cubes. Place the potatoes in a large bowl and gently stir in the salt, vinegar, celery, onion, green pepper and parsley.

MAYONNAISE

3 egg yolks, at room temperature
1 teaspoon lemon juice
1 tablespoon white-wine vinegar
1/4 teaspoon dry mustard
1 teaspoon salt
1/4 teaspoon white pepper
2 cups vegetable oil
3 hard-cooked eggs, sliced
2 tablespoons finely chopped fresh parsley

To make the mayonnaise, beat the egg yolks with a whisk or rotary or electric beater for 2 to 3 minutes until they thicken and cling to the beater. Add the lemon juice, vinegar, mustard, salt and pepper. Beat in the oil 1/2 teaspoon at a time until 1/4 cup is used, making sure each spoonful is absorbed. Still beating, slowly add the rest of the oil. Gently fold the mayonnaise into the potatoes. Taste for seasoning. Garnish with egg slices and chopped parsley.

Tomato Aspic

To serve 4 to 6

2 envelopes unflavored gelatin
½ cup cold beef stock, fresh or canned
2 tablespoons butter
¼ cup finely chopped onions
3 tablespoons tomato paste
4½ cups canned tomatoes with juice (2 one-pound, 3-ounce cans)
¾ teaspoon salt
¾ teaspoon sugar
½ teaspoon Worcestershire sauce
1 teaspoon finely chopped fresh tarragon or ½ teaspoon dried tarragon
1 teaspoon vegetable oil
1 cup mayonnaise combined with 2 tablespoons finely cut chives, or 1 cup sour cream combined with 1 tablespoon red caviar

Soften the gelatin in the cold beef stock for about 5 minutes. In a heavy 2- to 3-quart saucepan, melt the butter over moderate heat. When the foam subsides, add the onions and cook, stirring, for 4 or 5 minutes until they are transparent but not brown. Stir in the tomato paste, the canned tomatoes and the softened gelatin, and mix together until the ingredients are thoroughly combined.

Then add the salt, the sugar, Worcestershire sauce and the tarragon, and bring to a boil, stirring constantly. Reduce the heat to its lowest point and simmer the mixture with the pan partially covered for about 30 minutes. Rub the mixture through a fine sieve or food mill into a mixing bowl.

With a pastry brush or paper towel, lightly coat the inside of a 1-quart mold with the vegetable oil. Pour in the tomato mixture, let it cool slightly and then refrigerate for 2 to 3 hours, or until the aspic is firm. To unmold, run a knife around the inside surfaces of the mold and place a serving plate upside down on top of the mold. Grasping the plate and the mold together firmly, invert the two. Rap the plate firmly on a table, and the aspic should slide out onto the plate. Serve the tomato aspic as a salad course with mayonnaise mixed with finely cut chives, or with sour cream mixed with red caviar.

Caesar Salad

No one really knows how Caesar Salad got its name, but it is believed to have originated in Southern California in the 1920s.

To serve 4 to 6

2 medium-sized heads romaine lettuce
10 to 12 croutons, preferably made from French or Italian-style bread
4 to 8 tablespoons vegetable oil
1 teaspoon finely chopped garlic
2 eggs
1/8 teaspoon salt
1/8 teaspoon freshly ground black pepper
1/2 cup olive oil
4 tablespoons lemon juice
1 cup freshly grated Parmesan cheese
6 to 8 flat anchovies (optional)

Separate the romaine lettuce and wash the leaves under cold running water. Dry each leaf thoroughly with paper towels. Then wrap the lettuce in a dry kitchen towel and chill while you assemble the other ingredients. Cut a loaf of bread into 1 1/2-inch-thick slices. Trim the crusts and cut each slice into 1 1/2-inch squares. In a heavy skillet, large enough to hold all the croutons in one layer, heat 4 tablespoons of the vegetable oil over high heat until a light haze forms above it. Add the croutons and brown them on all sides, turning them with tongs, and, if necessary, add up to another 4 tablespoons of oil. Remove the pan from the heat, then add the chopped garlic and toss the croutons about in the hot fat. Remove the croutons to paper towels to drain, cool and crisp.

Plunge the eggs into rapidly boiling water for 10 seconds, remove and set aside. Break the chilled romaine into serving-sized pieces and scatter them in the bottom of a large salad bowl, preferably glass or porcelain. Add the salt, pepper and olive oil, and toss the lettuce with two large spoons or, better still, with your hands. Then break the eggs on top of the salad, add the lemon juice and mix again until the lettuce is thoroughly coated with the dressing. Add the cheese and the anchovies, if you are using them, and mix once more. Scatter the croutons over the top and serve at once on chilled salad plates.

Spinach Salad

To serve 4 to 6

½ pound uncooked young spinach
1 large cucumber
1 teaspoon salt
4 medium-sized stalks celery
¼ cup coarsely chopped black olives
½ cup pine nuts

Wash the spinach under cold running water, drain and pat thoroughly dry with paper towels. Strip the leaves from the stems and discard the stems along with any tough or discolored leaves. Peel the cucumber and slice it in half lengthwise. Run the tip of a teaspoon down the center to scrape out the seeds. Cut the halves into strips ¼ inch wide and then crosswise into ¼-inch dice. To rid the cucumber of excess moisture, in a small bowl mix the diced cucumber with 1 teaspoon of salt. Let it rest for 15 minutes to ½ hour, then drain the liquid that will accumulate and pat the cucumber dice dry with paper towels.

Trim the leaves and stems of the celery; wash the stalks under cold water and dry them thoroughly with paper towels. Cut each stalk in ¼-inch strips and then cut into ¼-inch dice. Toss the spinach, cucumber and celery in a salad bowl, preferably of glass, add the olives and nuts and toss again. Chill until ready to serve.

DRESSING

2 tablespoons red wine vinegar
½ teaspoon salt
Freshly ground black pepper
½ teaspoon dry mustard
6 tablespoons vegetable oil

For the dressing, with a whisk beat the vinegar, salt, pepper and mustard together in a small bowl. Still whisking, gradually pour in the oil and beat until the dressing is smooth and thick. Pour over the salad, toss until all the ingredients are thoroughly coated with the dressing and serve at once on chilled salad plates.

Avocado-Tomato Cocktail

To serve 4 to 6

1 ripe avocado, peeled and cut in ¼-inch dice
1 teaspoon lemon juice
2 medium-sized tomatoes, peeled, seeded and cut in ¼-inch dice
2 tablespoons minced onion
2 tablespoons finely chopped fresh parsley
1 teaspoon salt
Freshly ground black pepper
2 tablespoons red-wine vinegar
¼ cup vegetable oil

Cut the avocado in half, and, with a teaspoon, remove the seed and any brown tissuelike fibers clinging to the flesh. Remove the skin by stripping it off with your fingers, starting at the narrow, or stem, end (the dark-skinned variety does not peel as easily; use a small, sharp knife to pull away the skin if necessary). Dice the avocado and moisten it with the lemon juice to prevent discoloration. In a mixing bowl, combine the avocado, diced tomato and the minced onion. Add the parsley, salt and a few grindings of pepper, and gently mix the ingredients together.

With a whisk or fork, beat the vinegar and oil together, then pour it over the avocado-tomato mixture. Stir thoroughly again, then chill for at least an hour. Serve as a first course in chilled cocktail glasses or as a luncheon salad, arranged on a bed of crisp lettuce.

Three-Bean Salad

To serve 6 to 8

1 cup red kidney beans, freshly cooked or canned
1 cup white kidney beans, freshly cooked or canned
1 cup chick peas, freshly cooked or canned
¾ cup finely chopped onion or scallions
½ teaspoon finely chopped garlic
2 tablespoons finely chopped parsley
1 small green pepper, seeded and coarsely chopped (optional)
1 teaspoon salt
Freshly ground black pepper
3 tablespoons wine vinegar
½ cup olive oil

If you plan to use canned cooked beans and chick peas, drain them of all their canning liquid, wash them thoroughly under cold running water, drain again and pat dry with paper towels. If you plan to cook the beans yourself, follow the initial soaking directions for beans in the recipe for baked beans on page 17, and then cook them until tender. One half cup of dry uncooked beans yields approximately 1¼ cups cooked.

In a large bowl, combine the chick peas, red kidney beans and white kidney beans, the chopped onion or scallions, garlic, parsley and the chopped green pepper if you plan to use it.

Add the salt, a few grindings of pepper and the wine vinegar. Toss gently with a large spoon. Pour in the olive oil and toss again. This salad will be greatly improved if it is allowed to rest for at least an hour before serving it.

Bread and Butter Pickles

To make 4 to 5 pints

12 medium-sized cucumbers, cut into ¼-inch slices
1½ pounds onions, thinly sliced
½ cup salt
3 cups vinegar
3 cups sugar
½ teaspoon turmeric
¼ cup mustard seed
2 teaspoons celery seed
¼ teaspoon cayenne pepper

In a large glass or stainless-steel bowl, combine the sliced cucumbers, onions and salt. Let the mixture stand for 3 hours, then pour it into a colander to drain. Rinse with cold water, then drain again.

In an 8- to 10-quart saucepan, combine the vinegar, sugar, turmeric, mustard seed, celery seed and cayenne pepper. Bring to a boil and add the drained cucumber and onion slices. Reduce the heat to low, bring just to a simmer and simmer for 2 minutes. Avoid actual boiling to prevent the cucumber slices from softening too much. They should remain crisp.

Cool the pickles you want to serve immediately and pack the rest in hot, sterilized jars.

Baked Apples

To serve 6

6 large apples, such as Rome Beauty, York Imperial or Jonathan
1 cup sugar
2 cups boiling water
1 cinnamon stick
½ cup currants or raisins
½ cup chopped walnuts

Preheat the oven to 375°. Core each of the apples to within ½ inch of its base and arrange them in a buttered baking dish just large enough to hold them comfortably.

Combine the sugar, water and cinnamon stick in a saucepan, stir to dissolve the sugar, then bring to a boil. Boil rapidly for about 8 minutes, or until the mixture becomes a thin syrup.

In a mixing bowl, combine the currants or raisins with the chopped walnuts and stuff the centers of the apples with the mixture. Remove the cinnamon stick from the syrup, pour the syrup over the apples and bake them in the middle of the oven for 40 minutes, or until they are soft to the touch but not falling apart.

Transfer the apples to individual serving dishes and pour the syrup remaining in the baking dish over them.

Cranberry-Orange Relish

To make 1 quart

½ cup water
½ cup orange juice
1 cup granulated sugar
1 pound whole cranberries
2 tablespoons grated orange rind

In a 3- or 4-quart saucepan, stir the water, orange juice and sugar together until the sugar is thoroughly dissolved. Add the cranberries, bring to a boil and cook for 3 to 5 minutes, stirring occasionally, until the skins of the berries begin to pop and the berries are tender but not mushy. Do not overcook them.

Remove the pan from the heat and stir in the orange rind. Transfer the mixture to a serving bowl, let cool, and then chill for at least an hour or two before serving.

Old-fashioned Apple Butter

To make about 3 pints

4 pounds tart apples
2 cups cider
4 to 5 cups sugar
2 teaspoons cinnamon
1 teaspoon ground cloves
½ teaspoon ground allspice

Cut the apples into quarters but do not peel or seed them. Combine them with the cider in an enameled or stainless-steel pot. Bring the cider to a boil, then reduce the heat to its lowest point and cover the pot. Simmer the apples, stirring them occasionally, for about 25 minutes, or until they are soft. Remove from the heat and with the back of a wooden spoon, mash the apples through a sieve. Measure the pulp and transfer it to a 6- to 8-quart casserole or heavy saucepan. Add ½ cup of sugar for every cup of pulp, and add the cinnamon, cloves and allspice. Stirring occasionally, cook over medium heat about 4 hours, or until a tablespoon of the apple butter will stick to a saucer when the saucer is turned upside down. Ladle the apple butter that is to be stored into sterilized jars. Let it cool to room temperature, then seal it with paraffin and cover tightly.

Grandmother Brown's Rhubarb Marmalade

To make 3 pints

2 pounds rhubarb, coarsely chopped
¼ cup orange juice
¼ cup lemon juice
2 pounds sugar
2 oranges, peeled, seeded and sectioned
1 lemon, peeled, seeded and sectioned
Grated rind of 1 orange
Grated rind of 1 lemon
1½ cups walnuts, halved

Combine the rhubarb, orange juice and lemon juice in an enameled or stainless-steel saucepan. Bring to a boil, cover, reduce the heat and simmer for about an hour, or until the rhubarb is soft. Stir in the sugar and, stirring constantly, boil rapidly for about 5 minutes, or until the mixture is translucent and lightly holds its shape in a spoon. Turn off the heat, stir in the orange and lemon sections and rinds, and the walnuts. Still stirring occasionally, let the marmalade cool to room temperature, then pour it into sterilized glasses and seal with paraffin.

Meat

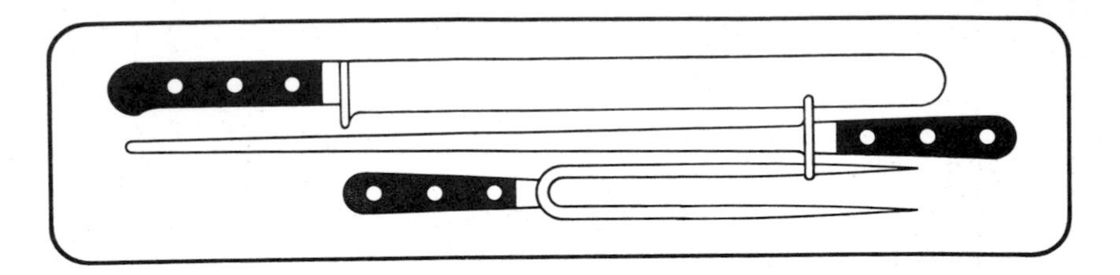

Roast Lamb Shanks and Lentils

To serve 4

- 2 cloves garlic cut into paper-thin slivers
- 4 meaty lamb shanks (about 1 pound each)
- Salt
- Freshly ground black pepper
- 3 tablespoons vegetable oil
- 2 tablespoons butter
- ½ cup finely chopped onion
- 2½ cups beef stock, fresh or canned
- 2½ cups lentils, thoroughly washed and drained
- 1 bay leaf
- ½ cup chopped scallions
- ¼ cup chopped fresh parsley

Preheat the oven to 350°. With the point of a small, sharp knife, insert 2 or 3 garlic slivers into the meaty portion of each lamb shank. Then sprinkle the shanks generously with salt and a few grindings of black pepper. In a 12-inch heavy skillet, heat the oil over high heat until a light haze forms over it. Add the shanks, and then, over moderate heat, cook them on all sides for about 10 minutes, turning them with tongs. When the shanks are a deep golden brown, transfer them to a rack set in a shallow roasting pan. Roast them in the middle of the oven for about an hour, or until the shanks are tender. Basting is unnecessary.

While the shanks are roasting, melt 2 tablespoons of butter over moderate heat in a 2- to 4-quart saucepan. When the foam subsides add the onions and cook them for about 6 minutes, stirring frequently until they are transparent but not brown. Pour in the stock and add the lentils, bay leaf, salt and a few grindings of black pepper. Bring to a boil. Cover the pot and reduce the heat to its lowest point. Simmer the lentils, stirring occasionally, for about 30 minutes, or until they have absorbed all the stock and are very tender.

To serve, stir into the lentils 2 tablespoons of drippings from the roasting pan and ½ cup of chopped scallions. Taste for seasoning. Arrange the lamb shanks and the lentils on a large, heated platter and sprinkle with parsley.

Crown Roast of Lamb with Peas and New Potatoes

To serve 6 to 8

A crown roast of lamb, consisting of 16 to 18 chops and weighing about 4½ pounds
1 clove garlic, cut into tiny slivers (optional)
2 teaspoons salt
1 teaspoon freshly ground black pepper
1 teaspoon crushed dried rosemary
16 to 18 peeled new potatoes, all about 1½ inches in diameter
3 cups cooked fresh or frozen peas
2 tablespoons melted butter
6 to 8 sprigs of fresh mint

Preheat the oven to 475°. With the point of a small, sharp knife make small incisions a few inches apart in the meaty portions of the lamb, and insert in them the slivers of garlic, if you are using it. Combine the salt, pepper and rosemary, and with your fingers pat the mixture all over the bottom and sides of the crown. To help keep its shape, stuff the crown with a crumpled sheet of foil and wrap the ends of the chop bones in strips of foil to prevent them from charring and snapping off. Place the crown of lamb on a small rack set in a shallow roasting pan just large enough to hold it comfortably and roast it in the center of the oven for about 20 minutes. Then turn down the heat to 400° and surround the crown with the new potatoes, basting them with the pan drippings and sprinkling them lightly with salt. Continue to roast the lamb (basting the lamb is unnecessary, but baste the potatoes every 15 minutes or so) for about an hour to an hour and 15 minutes, depending upon how well done you prefer your lamb. Ideally, it should be served when it is still somewhat pink, and should register 140° to 150° on a meat thermometer.

When the crown is done, carefully transfer it to a large circular platter, remove the foil and let the lamb rest about 10 minutes to make carving easier. Meanwhile, combine the peas with the melted butter and season them with as much salt as is necessary. Fill the hollow of the crown with as many of the peas as it will hold and serve any remaining peas separately. Put a paper frill on the end of each chop bone and surround the crown with the roasted potatoes. Garnish with mint and serve at once.

To carve the lamb, insert a large fork in the side of the crown to steady it and with a large, sharp knife cut down through each rib to detach the chops. Two rib chops per person is a customary portion.

Roast Mint-stuffed Leg of Lamb

To serve 8 to 10

A 6-pound leg of lamb, boned
4 slices bacon, cut into ½-inch pieces
1 cup coarsely chopped fresh mint
1 teaspoon finely chopped garlic
½ teaspoon salt
Freshly ground black pepper
4 tablespoons vegetable oil
2 large onions, thinly sliced
2 large carrots, thinly sliced
4 stalks celery, coarsely chopped
Salt
1½ cups beef or chicken stock, fresh or canned (optional)

Have the butcher bone a leg of lamb by removing the rump and leg bone, which will create a deep pocket for the stuffing. Ask him to leave the shank bone in. Although the effect will not be quite as impressive, the leg may be cut open and boned entirely. Do not remove the parchmentlike covering called the fell from the outside of the lamb.

For the stuffing, combine in a mixing bowl the bacon, chopped mint and garlic and stir into it ½ teaspoon of salt and a few grindings of black pepper. Fill the pocket with the stuffing and either sew the openings together or tightly skewer them. Or, if the leg has been cut open, lay it out flat, skin side down, and spread the stuffing over it. Roll the meat so as to enclose the stuffing completely, sew or skewer it, then tie it at 2-inch intervals so that it will hold its shape while cooking.

Preheat the oven to 475°. With a pastry brush or paper towel coat the lamb with the vegetable oil and place it fat side up on a rack set in a roasting pan just about large enough to hold it comfortably. Roast the lamb uncovered in the center of the oven for about 25 minutes. Then turn the heat down to 375° and scatter the onions, carrots and celery in the bottom of the pan. Sprinkle the lamb generously with salt and a few grindings of black pepper, and roast for about an hour for medium-rare lamb (140° to 150° on a meat thermometer) or up to ½ hour longer for well-done lamb (165° to 170°).

A simple pan gravy may be made by removing the lamb to a heated platter (the meat will be easier to carve if it rests for about 10 minutes) and pouring the 1½ cups of stock into the roasting pan. Bring it to a boil on top of the stove for about 3 minutes, meanwhile scraping into it any brown particles clinging to the bottom and sides of the pan. Strain it, discard the vegetables, and then skim the gravy of all its surface fat. Taste for seasoning and serve in a gravy boat with the carved lamb.

Crown Roast of Pork with Sausage-Apple Stuffing

To serve 10 to 12

STUFFING
3 tablespoons butter
3/4 cup finely chopped onion
1/4 cup finely chopped celery
1/2 cup peeled, cored and coarsely diced tart apples
1/2 cup fresh bread crumbs
1 pound ground pork (the crown roast trimmings plus extra pork, if necessary)
1/2 pound well-seasoned sausage meat
1/2 cup finely chopped parsley
1/2 teaspoon sage
1 1/2 teaspoons salt
Freshly ground black pepper

A crown roast of pork, consisting of 22 chops and weighing 8 to 9 pounds

Preheat the oven to 350°. For the stuffing, melt the butter over moderate heat in an 8- to 10-inch skillet. When the foam subsides, add the onion and cook, stirring frequently, for about 5 minutes, then add the celery and apples. Cook without browning about 5 minutes longer. Scrape the contents of the pan into a large mixing bowl. Add the bread crumbs, ground pork, sausage meat, parsley, sage, salt and a few grindings of black pepper. With a large spoon, mix all the ingredients gently but thoroughly together. Do not taste the uncooked stuffing, for it contains raw pork; instead, fry a small ball of the stuffing in the skillet. Then season the rest of the mixture with more salt and pepper if necessary.

Fill the center of the crown with the stuffing, mounding it slightly. Cover it with a round of foil and wrap the ends of the chop bones in strips of foil to prevent them from charring and snapping off. Place the crown on a rack in a shallow roasting pan just about large enough to hold it comfortably, and roast it in the center of the oven, undisturbed, for about 3 hours, or until a meat thermometer, if you have used one, reads 170° to 175°. One half hour before the pork is done, remove the circle of foil from the top of the stuffing to allow the top to brown.

Carefully transfer the crown to a large, heated, circular platter, strip the foil from the ends of the chops and replace it with paper frills. Let the crown rest for about 10 minutes before carving and serving.

To carve the pork, insert a large fork in the side of the crown to steady it and, with a large, sharp knife, cut down through each rib to detach the chops. Two chops per person is a customary portion, accompanied by a generous serving of the stuffing. Buttered peas would make a fine and colorful accompaniment.

Stuffed Pork Chops

To serve 6

STUFFING

1½ cups fine, dry bread crumbs
¼ cup heavy cream
2 tablespoons butter
¼ cup finely chopped onion
¼ teaspoon finely chopped garlic
½ pound well-seasoned sausage meat
⅛ teaspoon thyme
3 tablespoons finely chopped parsley
Salt
Freshly ground black pepper

To make the stuffing, combine the bread crumbs and cream in a small mixing bowl, and stir together to saturate the crumbs thoroughly. Over moderate heat, melt the 2 tablespoons of butter in an 8-inch skillet. When the foam subsides, add the onions, garlic and crumbled sausage meat. Stirring constantly, cook until the sausage has rendered most of its fat and has lightly browned. Scrape the contents of the pan into a sieve and let the excess fat drain through. Then combine the sausage meat mixture with the bread crumbs in the mixing bowl. Add the thyme and chopped parsley and mix together gently. Taste for seasoning. Add as much salt as you think it needs, and a little freshly ground pepper.

6 well-trimmed, center-cut loin pork chops, 1 inch thick, each chop slit on the side to create a pocket about 3 inches deep
Salt
Freshly ground black pepper
4 tablespoons vegetable oil
½ cup finely chopped onion
½ cup finely chopped, scraped carrot
¼ teaspoon thyme
1 tablespoon flour
1 cup chicken stock, fresh or canned

Preheat the oven to 325°. With a small spoon, pack as much of the stuffing as you can into the pork chop pockets and seal the openings with small skewers. Sprinkle the chops generously on both sides with salt and a few grindings of black pepper. Heat 4 tablespoons of oil over high heat in a 10- or 12-inch heavy skillet until a light haze forms over it. Add the chops and cook them on each side for about 3 minutes, regulating the heat so that they brown easily and quickly without burning. Remove them to a platter. Pour off all but a thin film of fat from the skillet and add the ½ cup of chopped onion, carrot and thyme. Cook over moderate heat for 5 to 8 minutes until the vegetables color lightly. Then mix in the tablespoon of flour, add the stock and bring it to a boil. Stirring constantly, cook until the stock thickens lightly. Place the browned chops, and any liquid which has accumulated around them, in this mixture.

Cover tightly, and bake in the middle of the oven, basting occasionally with the pan juices, for 30 to 40 minutes, or until tender.

To serve, arrange the chops on a heated platter and pour the sauce, strained or not, as you prefer, over them.

Baked Bourbon-glazed Ham

To serve 12 to 14

A 12- to 14-pound smoked ham, processed, precooked variety
3/4 cup bourbon whiskey
2 cups dark brown sugar
1 tablespoon dry mustard
3/4 cup whole cloves
2 navel oranges, peeled and sectioned

Preheat the oven to 325°. Place the ham fat side up on a rack set in a shallow roasting pan large enough to hold the ham comfortably. Bake in the middle of the oven, without basting, for two hours, or until the meat can be easily pierced with a fork. For greater cooking certainty, insert a meat thermometer in the fleshiest part of the ham before baking it. It should register between 130° and 140° when the ham is done.

When the ham is cool enough to handle comfortably, cut away the rind with a large, sharp knife. Then score the ham by cutting deeply through the fat until you reach the meat, making the incisions 1/2 inch apart lengthwise and crosswise. Return the ham to the rack in the pan and raise the oven heat to 450°. With a pastry brush, paint the ham on all sides with 1/2 cup of the whiskey. Then combine the sugar and mustard and 1/4 cup of whiskey, and pat the mixture firmly into the scored fat. Stud the fat at the intersections or in the center of each diamond with a whole clove, and arrange the orange sections as decoratively as you can on the top of the ham with toothpicks or small skewers to secure them. Baste lightly with the drippings on the bottom of the pan and bake the ham undisturbed in the hot oven for 15 to 20 minutes, or until the sugar has melted and formed a brilliant glaze.

Sweetbreads and Ham under Glass

To serve 6

6 pairs sweetbreads, about 3 pounds
2 tablespoons lemon juice
2 teaspoons salt
2 cups water
2/3 cup sherry
6 tablespoons butter
12 unpeeled mushroom caps, 1 1/2 to 2 inches in diameter, rubbed lightly with a damp paper towel

SAUCE
1/2 cup sherry
1 cup heavy cream
2 teaspoons lemon juice
Salt
White pepper

6 circles of white bread, 3 1/2 inches in diameter, lightly browned on both sides in 4 tablespoons of hot butter
6 slices cooked ham, 1/4 inch thick, cut into circles 3 1/2 inches in diameter

To prepare the sweetbreads for poaching, soak them for about 2 hours in enough cold water to cover them, changing the water every 45 minutes or so. Then soak again, for another hour, in 2 quarts of cold water mixed with 2 tablespoons of lemon juice and 2 teaspoons salt. Drain. Separate the sweetbread lobes, and cut away and discard the soft, white connecting tubes. With a small, sharp knife, pull off as much of the thin outside membrane of the sweetbreads as you can without tearing the delicate flesh.

Place the sweetbreads in a 2-quart enameled or stainless-steel saucepan, and add 2 cups of water and 2/3 cup of sherry. If the liquid doesn't quite cover the sweetbreads, add more water. Bring to a simmer over moderate heat, then lower the heat and cook as slowly as possible, uncovered, for about 15 minutes. Drain, plunge into cold water for 5 minutes, then drain again. Pat dry with paper towels.

Over moderate heat, melt 4 tablespoons of the butter in a 10-inch enameled or stainless-steel skillet, and when the foam subsides add the sweetbreads. Cook them on each side for about 3 minutes, or until they are a delicate brown. Remove to a platter. Melt the remaining butter in the skillet and cook the mushrooms briskly for a minute or two on each side to brown them lightly, then put them aside with the sweetbreads. Pour off all but a thin film of the butter from the pan and pour in the 1/2 cup of sherry. Over high heat, boil briskly for 2 minutes, then add the cream and boil rapidly for about 5 minutes, or until it thickens enough to coat a spoon. Add the lemon juice and season with as much salt and white pepper as you think it needs. Put it aside. Preheat the oven to 375°.

Arrange the toast rounds in individual 4- to 5-inch shallow ramekins. Top each round with a slice of ham, then a pair of sweetbreads and, finally, the mushroom caps. Pour equal amounts of the sauce over each cap and cover with individual glass bells. Heat in the middle of the oven for 12 to 15 minutes and serve at once.

Barbecued Spareribs

To serve 4 to 6

1/4 cup vegetable oil
1 teaspoon garlic, minced
2 medium onions, finely chopped
1 six-ounce can tomato paste
1/4 cup white vinegar
1 teaspoon salt
1 teaspoon basil or thyme
1/4 cup strained honey
1/2 cup beef stock
1/2 cup Worcestershire sauce
1 teaspoon dry mustard
4 pounds spareribs

Heat the vegetable oil over high heat in a 10- or 12-inch skillet. When a light haze forms above it, add the garlic and onions, and cook, stirring frequently, for 3 to 4 minutes without letting the onions brown. Combine the tomato paste and the vinegar, and then add it to the skillet. Stir in the salt, basil or thyme, the honey, beef stock, Worcestershire sauce and mustard. Mix thoroughly and simmer uncovered over low heat for 10 to 15 minutes. Remove from heat. Preheat the oven to 400°. Place the spareribs fat side up on a rack set in a shallow roasting pan and with a pastry brush thoroughly coat the surface of the meat with the barbecue sauce. Bake in the middle of the oven for 45 minutes to 1 hour, basting thoroughly with the barbecue sauce every 10 minutes or so. When the spareribs are brown and crisp, cut into individual portions and serve at once.

Ham Balls

To make 32 ham balls

1 cup fresh bread crumbs
3 tablespoons milk
1 pound fresh lean pork, finely ground, combined with ½ pound cooked smoked ham, finely ground
1 tablespoon prepared mustard
1 tablespoon finely chopped fresh parsley
1 egg, lightly beaten
Freshly ground black pepper
2 tablespoons butter
2 tablespoons vegetable oil
¾ cup dry red wine

Soak the bread crumbs in the milk for about 5 minutes, then combine them with the ground pork and ham in a large mixing bowl. Add the mustard, parsley, lightly beaten egg and a few grindings of black pepper, and with a large spoon mix them thoroughly together. Form the mixture into small balls about 1 inch in diameter and chill for at least ½ hour.

Preheat the oven to 350°. Over high heat, melt the butter with the oil in a large, heavy skillet. When the foam subsides, add the ham balls. To help keep their shape as they brown, roll the balls around in the hot fat by shaking the pan back and forth over the burner. When the ham balls are well browned on all sides (this should take about 5 minutes), transfer them with a slotted spoon to a 2-quart casserole. Pour off all but a thin film of fat from the skillet and pour in the wine. Bring it to a boil over high heat, scraping and stirring into it any brown bits clinging to the bottom and sides of the pan. Cook briskly for about a minute, then pour the wine into the casserole. Cover tightly and bake in the middle of the oven for about 30 minutes, basting the ham balls after 15 minutes with the wine. Serve either directly from the casserole or arrange the balls on a heated platter and pour the sauce over them. Or, place the ham balls and sauce in a chafing dish and serve, speared with decorative tooth picks, as an accompaniment to cocktails.

Braised Short Ribs of Beef

To serve 6 to 8

5 to 6 pounds lean short ribs of beef, cut into 3- to 4-inch pieces
Salt
Freshly ground black pepper
½ cup flour
2 tablespoons butter
1 cup coarsely chopped onion
1 cup coarsely chopped, scraped carrot
½ teaspoon finely chopped garlic
⅛ teaspoon thyme
1 cup beef stock, fresh or canned
2 small bay leaves

Preheat the oven to 500°. Season the short ribs generously with salt and a few grindings of black pepper. Dip them in flour, vigorously shaking off any excess, then arrange them side by side on a rack in a shallow roasting pan. Brown them in the middle of the oven for 20 to 25 minutes, checking periodically to make sure they do not burn.

Meanwhile, melt the 2 tablespoons of butter over moderate heat in a heavy, 6-quart, flameproof casserole. When the foam subsides, add the onion, carrot, garlic and thyme, and, stirring frequently, cook for 6 to 8 minutes until the vegetables are lightly colored. Place the browned ribs, preferably in one layer, on top of the vegetables, add the stock to the roasting pan and stir into it any brown bits clinging to the pan. Then pour it over the ribs in the casserole. Bring to a boil on top of the stove, add the bay leaves and cover the casserole tightly. Reduce the oven heat to 325°. Braise the short ribs in the middle of the oven for about an hour until the meat shows no resistance when pierced with a fork.

To serve, arrange the short ribs on a heated platter. Strain the braising juices through a fine sieve into a saucepan, pressing down on the vegetables to extract all their juices before discarding them. Skim the fat from the surface, taste the sauce for seasoning and pour over the meat.

Roast Beef

A GUIDE TO ROASTING A STANDING RIB ROAST

There are two American methods for cooking a rib roast successfully, and each one has its partisans. The first is the searing method, in which the roast is seared in a 450° oven for 20 to 30 minutes, the oven then turned down to 250° and the roast cooked to the desired degree of doneness. The second is the low-, constant-temperature method, in which the roast is cooked in a 300° to 325° oven. In either of these procedures the following points should be kept in mind.

1. Salt and pepper may be sprinkled over the roast before, during or after the roasting period.
2. It is unnecessary to use a rack for a standing rib roast, since the ribs of the roast form a natural rack. Roast the ribs, fat side up, in a shallow roasting pan a little larger than the roast itself.
3. No water or any other liquid should be added to the roast during the cooking period. Nor should it be covered or basted at any time.
4. For predictable results, a good meat thermometer (preferably a professional cook's thermometer, which begins at 0° rather than 140°) is imperative. How long the beef has been aged, the width of the so-called "eye" (the meaty heart of the rib) and the accuracy of the oven are factors which cause unpredictable variations in cooking times. Insert the meat thermometer so that its tip is directly in the center of the roast. It should not touch bone or rest in fat. The roasting-time chart which follows is at best only an approximate gauge.

TIMETABLES FOR ROASTING A STANDING RIB ROAST

WEIGHT: 6 TO 8 POUNDS	OVEN TEMPERATURE: 300° TO 325°
INTERNAL TEMPERATURE WHEN DONE	COOKING TIME MINUTES PER POUND
130° to 140° (rare)	20
150° to 160° (medium)	25
160° to 170° (well done)	30

Ideally, a standing rib roast (or, for that matter, any other roast) should be allowed to rest outside the oven for at least 10 minutes before carving. Since the meat will continue to cook internally as it stands, remove it from the oven when the meat thermometer reads 10° lower than the temperature you desire. As the roast rests, the surface juices will retreat back into the meat, carving will be easier, and the beef juicier and better textured. To carve, first remove a thin slice of beef from the large end of the roast so that it will stand firmly on this end. Insert a large fork below the top rib and carve slices of beef from the top, separating each slice as you proceed down along the rib bone.

New England Boiled Dinner

To serve 6

- 4 pounds corned beef
- 2 pounds green cabbage, cored and quartered
- 12 to 16 new potatoes, about 1½ inches in diameter, peeled
- 6 small carrots, scraped
- 12 small white onions, about 1 inch in diameter, peeled and trimmed
- 6 medium-sized beets
- 2 tablespoons finely chopped parsley

Before cooking the corned beef, ask your butcher whether it should be soaked in water to remove some of the salt. If it has been mildly cured, soaking will not be necessary.

Place the corned beef in a 5- or 6-quart pot and cover it with enough cold water to rise at least 2 inches above the top of the meat. Bring to a boil, skimming off any scum that rises to the surface. Half cover the pot, turn the heat to its lowest point (the liquid should barely simmer) and cook the beef from 4 to 6 hours, or until tender. If necessary, add more hot water to the pot from time to time to keep the meat constantly covered.

Cook the cabbage separately in boiling salted water for about 15 minutes. The potatoes, carrots and onions may be cooked together in a pot of salted boiling water of their own. The beets, however, require different treatment. Scrub them thoroughly, then cut off their tops, leaving 1 inch of stem. Cover them with boiling water and bring to a boil. Simmer the beets from ½ to 1½ hours, or until they are tender. Let them cool a bit, then slip off their skins.

To serve the dinner in the traditional way, slice the corned beef and arrange it along the center of a large heated platter. Surround the meat with the vegetables and sprinkle the vegetables with chopped parsley. Horseradish, mustard and a variety of pickles make excellent accompaniments to this hearty meal.

NOTE: In New England the vegetables, other than the beets, are often added to the simmering corned beef during the last half hour or so of cooking. For some tastes, however, the briny flavor imparted to the vegetables by the corned beef detracts from their natural flavors.

Red-Flannel Hash

To serve 4 to 6

¼ pound bacon, cut in ¼-inch pieces
½ cup finely chopped onion
2 cups (about 1 pound) finely chopped, cooked corn beef *(see New England Boiled Dinner, page 39)*
1 cup diced cooked beets, fresh or canned
3 cups coarsely chopped cooked potatoes
4 tablespoons finely chopped fresh parsley
¼ cup heavy cream
Salt
Freshly ground black pepper

In a 10- or 12-inch skillet, preferably of the nonstick variety, fry the bacon until brown but not too crisp. Then set it aside to drain on paper towels. Pour off all but 2 tablespoons of fat from the pan and reserve. Add the onions and cook them over moderate heat for 3 to 5 minutes, but don't let them brown. Scrape them into a large mixing bowl. Add the corned beef, beets, the reserved bacon, potatoes, 2 tablespoons of chopped parsley and the cream. Mix together gently but thoroughly, taste for seasoning, and add salt and freshly ground pepper to taste.

Heat the bacon fat reserved in the skillet. Add the hash, and, with a spatula, spread it evenly in the pan and pat it down. Cook uncovered over moderate heat for 35 to 40 minutes, shaking the pan occasionally to prevent the hash from sticking. As it cooks, remove any excess fat from the top or sides of the pan with a spoon or bulb baster. When the hash is done (it should be crusty brown on the bottom) slide a metal spatula around the inside edge of the skillet and as far under the hash as you can without crumbling it. Then place a large, round platter over the skillet, and, gripping platter and skillet firmly together, invert the hash onto the platter.

If any of the hash has stuck to the pan, lift it out with a spatula and patch it in place. Sprinkle with the remaining chopped parsley and serve with poached eggs if desired.

Chili con Carne

To serve 6 to 8

3 pounds top round, cut into ½-inch cubes
6 tablespoons vegetable oil
2 cups coarsely chopped onion
2 tablespoons finely chopped garlic
4 tablespoons chili powder
1 teaspoon oregano
1 teaspoon ground cumin
1 teaspoon red-pepper flakes
1 six-ounce can tomato paste
4 cups beef stock, fresh or canned
1 teaspoon salt
Freshly ground black pepper
1½ cups freshly cooked red kidney beans or drained canned kidney beans (optional)

Pat the meat dry with paper towels. Then, in a 12-inch heavy skillet, heat 4 tablespoons of the oil until a light haze forms above it. Add the meat and cook over high heat for 2 to 3 minutes, stirring, until the meat is lightly browned. With a slotted spoon transfer it to a 4-quart heavy flameproof casserole. Add the remaining 2 tablespoons of oil to the skillet and in it cook the onion and garlic for 4 to 5 minutes, stirring frequently.

Remove the skillet from the heat, add the 4 tablespoons chili powder, or to taste, oregano, cumin and pepper flakes, and stir until the onions are well coated with the mixture. Then add the tomato paste, pour in the beef stock and with a large spoon mix the ingredients together thoroughly before adding them to the meat in the casserole. Add the salt and a few grindings of black pepper. Bring to a boil, stirring once or twice, then half cover the pot, turn the heat to low and simmer for 1 to 1½ hours, or until the meat is tender.

If you plan to use the beans, add them to the casserole 15 minutes or so before the meat is done or, if you prefer, serve the chili with the three-bean salad on page 24. In either case, before serving the chili, skim it of as much of the surface fat as you can. If the chili is refrigerated overnight, the fat will rise to the surface and can be easily skimmed off before reheating.

NOTE: Chile con carne is often made with coarsely ground chuck in place of the cubed round steak. Follow the above recipe, but be sure to break up the ground chuck with a fork as you brown it.

Roast Saddle of Venison with Cream Sauce

To serve 6 to 8

4 tablespoons black peppercorns
A 5-pound saddle of venison
2 teaspoons salt
10 tablespoons melted butter
4 to 6 cups beef stock, fresh or canned

Preheat the oven to 475°. Crush the peppercorns in a mortar with a pestle or wrap them in a kitchen towel and press a rolling pin back and forth over them. The peppercorns should be quite coarse, not reduced to a powder. Sprinkle the meat with the salt, then with the heel of your hand press as much of the crushed pepper as you can into the meat. Place the meat on a rack in a shallow roasting pan large enough to hold it comfortably and pour 4 tablespoons of the melted butter over it. Pour 4 cups of the beef stock into the bottom of the pan. Roast the venison, uncovered, in the middle of the oven for 15 minutes, then pour 2 more tablespoons of butter over the meat and reduce the oven heat to 425°. Continue roasting, basting occasionally with the rest of the butter for 1½ hours longer. (If the saddle is young and tender, and you prefer game rare, roast only 1 hour longer.) Add the remaining stock to the pan, ½ cup at a time, if at any point the pan drippings have evaporated.

SAUCE
2 tablespoons butter
2 tablespoons flour
2 tablespoons currant jelly
½ cup heavy cream

When the venison is done, transfer it to a heated platter and let it rest while you make the sauce. In a 1- to 2-quart enameled or stainless-steel saucepan, melt 2 tablespoons of butter over moderate heat. When the foam subsides, stir in the flour. Cook over low heat, stirring constantly for a minute or so or until the mixture bubbles up and froths. Pour in 2 cups of the roasting pan juices (if there isn't enough, add to it as much stock or water as necessary). Bring to a boil, stirring constantly with a whisk until the sauce is smooth and slightly thickened. Reduce the heat to moderate and beat in the currant jelly and heavy cream. Simmer 2 or 3 minutes longer until the jelly is thoroughly dissolved. Taste for seasoning. Pour into a heated gravy boat and serve with the venison.

Fried Rabbit with Sour Cream Gravy

To serve 4

A 2½- to 3-pound fresh rabbit or defrosted frozen rabbit, cut in serving pieces
Salt
Freshly ground black pepper
1 cup flour
4 tablespoons butter
4 tablespoons vegetable oil
¼ cup finely chopped onion
1 teaspoon finely chopped garlic
1 cup chicken stock, fresh or canned
1 cup sour cream

Wash the rabbit pieces under cold running water and dry them thoroughly with paper towels. Sprinkle each piece generously with salt and a few grindings of pepper. Place the flour in a sturdy paper bag and drop the rabbit pieces into it, a few at a time. Shake the bag vigorously until each piece is thoroughly coated with flour, then remove the rabbit from the bag and shake the pieces free of excess flour. Set aside on wax paper.

In a heavy skillet large enough to hold all the pieces comfortably, heat the butter and oil over moderate heat. When the foam subsides, add the pieces of rabbit and cook them for 6 to 7 minutes on each side, turning them with tongs. When all the rabbit pieces are brown, cover the skillet and turn the heat to its lowest point. Cook the rabbit for 35 to 40 minutes, or until the flesh shows no resistance when pierced with the tip of a small, sharp knife. Arrange the pieces of rabbit attractively on a large heated platter and cover loosely with foil to keep them warm.

Pour off all but a thin film of fat from the skillet, add the chopped onion and garlic, and cook for 4 to 5 minutes over medium heat until the onions are lightly colored. Pour in the chicken stock, stirring in any brown bits that cling to the pan, and bring to a rapid boil.

Boil briskly until the stock reduces by about ⅓, then turn the heat down and, with a whisk, slowly beat in the sour cream. Simmer only long enough to heat the gravy through. Taste for seasoning and pour over the rabbit. Or, if you like, serve the gravy separately in a sauceboat.

Poultry

Roast Wild Turkey with Cornbread Stuffing

To serve 8 to 10

CORNBREAD STUFFING
10 tablespoons butter
1½ cups finely chopped onion
1 pound well-seasoned sausage meat
The turkey liver
6 cups coarsely crumbled cornbread made from cornbread recipe on page 87, omitting the sugar
½ teaspoon salt
Freshly ground black pepper
2 teaspoons thyme
¼ cup finely chopped fresh parsley
¼ cup Madeira or sherry
¼ cup heavy cream

CORNBREAD STUFFING: Melt 8 tablespoons of the butter in a large, heavy skillet, add the chopped onions and cook over moderate heat for 6 to 8 minutes, or until they color lightly. Scrape them into a large mixing bowl. Add the sausage to the skillet, now set over medium heat, and break the meat up with a fork as it cooks. When the meat is lightly browned, transfer it to a sieve set over a small bowl and let the fat drain through. Meanwhile, again in the same pan, melt the remaining 2 tablespoons of butter and, when the foam subsides, add the turkey liver. Brown it over high heat for 2 to 3 minutes, then chop it coarsely and combine with the onions in the bowl. Add the drained sausage meat, cornbread crumbs, salt, a few grindings of black pepper, the thyme and parsley. With a large spoon, gently stir the ingredients together, then moisten the stuffing with the Madeira or sherry and cream. Taste for seasoning.

TURKEY
A 10- to 12-pound wild turkey
1 teaspoon salt
Freshly ground black pepper
12 tablespoons melted butter (1½ quarter-pound sticks)
½ cup coarsely chopped onion

TURKEY: Preheat the oven to 350°. Wash the turkey under cold running water and dry it thoroughly inside and out with paper towels. Rub the inside of the turkey with the salt and a few grindings of pepper, and fill the body and breast cavities loosely with the stuffing, closing the openings with skewers or sewing them with thread. Truss the bird securely. With a pastry brush or paper towel, brush the outside of the turkey with a few tablespoons of the melted butter and sprinkle it with salt. Place the bird on a rack in a shallow roasting pan and scatter the onions around it in the bottom of the pan. Roast the turkey uncovered in the middle of the oven for about 2 hours, basting it every 15 minutes or so with the rest of the melted butter and with the drippings that accumulate in the pan.

To test for doneness pierce the thigh of the bird with the tip of a small, sharp knife. The juice should spurt out a clear yellow; if it is slightly pink, roast the bird for another 5 to 10 minutes. Transfer the turkey to a heated platter and let it rest for 10 minutes before carving.

GRAVY

3 tablespoons flour
1 cup water or chicken stock, fresh or canned
½ cup light cream
White pepper
Salt

While the turkey is resting, make the gravy. Pour off all but about 3 tablespoons of fat from the roasting pan and stir the flour into the pan. When the flour is thoroughly absorbed, add the cup of water or stock. Bring to a boil over high heat, stirring constantly with a wire whisk and incorporating into the liquid the brown sediment on the bottom and sides of the pan. When the sauce is quite thick, beat in the cream. If you prefer the gravy thinner, add a little more cream. Taste for seasoning and pour into a heated gravy boat. The gravy may be strained if you like.

NOTE: A domestic turkey may be stuffed and roasted in the same fashion as a wild turkey but may take 15 minutes or so longer to roast. Use the same test for doneness as described above.

Southern Fried Chicken with Cream Gravy

To serve 4

A 2½-pound frying chicken, cut into serving pieces
Salt
1 cup flour
1 cup lard, or ½ cup vegetable shortening combined with ½ cup lard

Wash the chicken pieces under cold running water and pat them thoroughly dry with paper towels. Sprinkle the pieces with salt on all sides. Put the cup of flour in a sturdy paper bag. Drop the chicken into the bag a few pieces at a time and shake the bag until each piece is thoroughly coated with flour. Remove the chicken pieces from the bag and vigorously shake them free of all excess flour. Lay them side by side on a sheet of wax paper. Preheat the oven to 200° and in the middle of the oven place a shallow baking dish.

Over high heat melt the lard or combined lard and shortening in a 10- or 12-inch heavy skillet. The fat should be ¼ inch deep. If it is not, add a little more. When a light haze forms above it, add the chicken pieces, starting them skin side down. It is preferable to begin frying the legs and thighs first, since they will take longer to cook than the breasts and wings. Cover the pan and fry the chicken over moderate heat for about 6 to 8 minutes, checking every now and then to make sure the chicken does not burn. When the pieces are deep brown on one side, turn them over and cover the pan again. Transfer the finished chicken to the baking dish in the oven and continue frying until all the pieces are cooked. Keep the chicken warm in the oven while you make the gravy.

CREAM GRAVY
2 tablespoons flour
¾ cup chicken stock, fresh or canned
½ to ¾ cup light cream
Salt
White pepper

Pour off all but 2 tablespoons of fat in the frying pan. Add 2 tablespoons of flour, and stir until the fat and flour are well combined. Pour in the chicken stock and ½ cup of the light cream, and cook over moderate heat, beating with a whisk until the gravy is smooth and thick. If it is too thick for your taste, stir in the remaining cream to thin it. Strain it through a fine sieve if you wish. Taste for seasoning, then pour into a heated gravy boat and serve with the fried chicken arranged attractively on a heated serving platter.

Smothered Chicken with Mushrooms

To serve 4

A 3-pound frying chicken, cut into serving pieces
Salt
Freshly ground black pepper
3 tablespoons butter
2 tablespoons vegetable oil
4 tablespoons finely chopped onion
3 tablespoons flour
1½ cups chicken stock, fresh or canned
½ pound mushrooms, thinly sliced
½ cup heavy cream

Preheat the oven to 350°. Wash the chicken under cold running water and pat the pieces thoroughly dry with paper towels. If they are damp, they will not brown well. Season them generously with salt and a few grindings of black pepper. In a heavy 10- or 12-inch skillet, melt the butter and the oil over high heat. When the foam subsides, brown the chicken pieces, a few at a time, starting them skin side down and turning them with tongs. Regulate the heat so that the chicken browns quickly without burning. Then transfer the pieces to a shallow casserole large enough to hold the chicken comfortably in 1 layer. To the fat remaining in the skillet, add the onions, and cook them, stirring occasionally, for about 5 minutes, or until they are soft and lightly colored. Stir in the flour, mix well with a spoon and pour in the chicken stock. Stirring constantly with a whisk, bring the stock to a boil, then turn down the heat and simmer for 2 to 3 minutes. Pour the sauce over the chicken in the casserole, cover tightly and cook in the center of the oven for about 20 minutes. Then scatter the sliced mushrooms around the chicken, basting them well with the pan gravy. Cook, covered, for another 10 minutes until the chicken is tender but not falling apart.

To serve, arrange the chicken attractively on a deep serving platter. Skim the gravy of as much of the surface fat as you can and stir in the cream. Simmer a minute or two on top of the stove, stirring constantly. Taste for seasoning and pour over the chicken.

Old-fashioned Chicken Pie

To serve 6 to 8

PASTRY
1¼ cups flour
4 tablespoons vegetable shortening or lard
2 tablespoons chilled butter, cut in ¼-inch pieces
⅛ teaspoon salt
3 tablespoons ice water

In a large mixing bowl, combine the flour, vegetable shortening or lard, butter and salt. Working quickly, use your fingertips to rub flour and fat together until they look like flakes of coarse meal. Pour the ice water over the mixture, toss together, and press and knead gently with your hands until the dough can be gathered into a compact ball. Dust very lightly with flour, wrap in wax paper and chill for at least ½ hour, or until you are about to make the pie.

A 5-pound roasting chicken, securely trussed
4 quarts chicken stock, fresh or canned, or half chicken stock and half water combined
½ teaspoon salt
12 to 16 small white onions, peeled, about 1 inch in diameter
4 large carrots, scraped and sliced, about 1 inch thick
8 tablespoons butter (1 quarter-pound stick), cut into small pieces
⅔ cup flour
½ cup heavy cream
1 tablespoon melted, cooled butter

Place the chicken in an 8-quart soup pot and cover it with the chicken stock or chicken stock and water. Add the ½ teaspoon of salt and bring the stock to a boil over high heat. Skim off all scum and froth as it rises to the surface. Partially cover the pan, reduce the heat to low and simmer the chicken, undisturbed, for about 1½ hours, or until tender but not falling apart. Remove the chicken and set it aside to cool.

Meanwhile, add the peeled onions and sliced carrots to the stock. Simmer, half covered, for about 20 minutes, or until the vegetables can be easily pierced with the point of a small, sharp knife. Remove them with a slotted spoon to a small bowl. Carefully remove and discard the skin from the chicken and cut the meat away from the bones. Cut the pieces into 1½- to 2-inch chunks. In a small saucepan, melt the butter over moderate heat without browning it. Off the heat, stir in the flour and mix until smooth. Skim the fat from the stock, then, in a slow stream pour 5 cups into the saucepan, stirring with a whisk all the while. Return the pan to moderate heat and cook, whisking constantly, until the sauce is thick and smooth. Stir in the cream and taste for seasoning.

Preheat the oven to 375°. Pour the sauce into a baking dish approximately 9 by 12 by 2 inches. Add the chicken, onions and carrots, and spread them out evenly. Then roll the dough on a lightly floured surface into a rectangle about 10 by 13 inches. Lift it up on a rolling pin and drape it over the top of the pan. Crimp the pastry around the sides of the pan to seal and secure it, and brush it with the tablespoon of melted butter. Make 2 small slits in the pastry to allow the steam to escape and bake the pie in the middle of the oven for about 45 minutes, or until the crust is golden brown.

Chicken Salad

To serve 4 to 6

4 cups cooked chicken *(see recipe opposite)*, cooled and cut into ½-inch dice
1 teaspoon salt
Freshly ground black pepper
3 tablespoons finely chopped onion or scallions
½ cup finely chopped celery, including some of the leaves
3 tablespoons capers, washed, drained and coarsely chopped
1 cup freshly made mayonnaise *(page 80)* or a good, unsweetened commercial variety
1 cup sour cream
1 tablespoon finely chopped parsley

Combine the chicken, salt and a few grindings of black pepper in a large mixing bowl. Stir in the onion or scallions, the celery and the capers. Mix together the mayonnaise and sour cream, and carefully fold it into the chicken mixture. Taste for seasoning. The chicken salad will gain in flavor if it is allowed to rest for an hour or so in the refrigerator before serving. Serve on individual chilled plates on crisp lettuce, or arrange the salad on a large, lettuce-lined platter. In either case, sprinkle the salad with the chopped parsley before serving.

Duck in Orange Aspic with Orange and Onion Salad

To serve 6

A 5- to 6-pound duck, cut into quarters
Duck giblets
4 cups orange juice, fresh or frozen
4 cups chicken stock, fresh or canned
1 cup thinly sliced onion
½ cup thinly sliced carrot
¾ cup celery, cut into 2-inch pieces
Herb bouquet of 6 sprigs parsley and 1 bay leaf, tied together
½ teaspoon thyme

In a 4- or 5-quart casserole combine the duck, giblets, orange juice and chicken stock. Bring to a boil, skim off all the surface scum and froth, then add the onion, carrot, celery, herb bouquet and thyme. Season with salt if you think it necessary. Half cover the casserole, reduce the heat to its lowest point and simmer the duck for about 1½ hours, or until tender. Then cut the skin and duck meat away from the bones and return the skin and bones to the casserole. Simmer the broth about ½ hour longer. Cut the duck meat into ½- by ¾-inch pieces and refrigerate.

ASPIC
2 envelopes unflavored gelatin
½ cup cold chicken stock or water
10 whole peppercorns
Peel of 2 oranges, coarsely chopped
2 teaspoons lemon juice
2 egg whites
Peel of 2 navel oranges cut into tiny slivers and blanched

THE ASPIC: Strain the entire contents of the casserole broth through a fine sieve, pressing down on the vegetables and duck parts to extract all their liquid before throwing them away. Measure the broth. You should have 4 cups. If less, add chicken stock; if more, boil down rapidly to 4 cups. Skim the surface of the broth of every bit of fat you can (this is easier if you chill the broth first until the fat rises and congeals on the surface), then return the broth to a 3- or 4-quart saucepan. Soften the gelatin in the ½ cup of cold stock or water for 5 minutes, then stir it into the broth. To clarify the aspic, add the peppercorns, the coarsely chopped orange peel and the lemon juice, then beat the egg whites to a froth with a wire whisk and whisk them into the broth. Bring to a boil over moderate heat, whisking constantly. When the aspic begins to froth and rise, remove the pan from the heat. Let it rest 5 minutes, then strain it into a deep bowl through a fine sieve lined with a dampened kitchen towel. Allow all the aspic to drain through without disturbing it at any point. The aspic should now be brilliantly clear. Taste for seasoning and add salt if necessary. Pour the aspic into a 1½-quart ring mold and set the mold in a bowl in crushed ice. Stir with a metal spoon until it becomes thick and syrupy (don't allow it to set), then mix into it the duck meat and slivers of orange peel. Refrigerate at least 2 hours, or until firmly set.

When you are ready to serve it, run a thin, sharp knife around the insides of the mold (including the cone), and dip the bottom in hot water for a few seconds. Then wipe the outside of the mold dry, place a large, chilled, circular serving plate upside down over the mold and, grasping both firmly, quickly turn plate and mold over. Rap them sharply on the table and the aspic should slide out. If it doesn't, repeat the process.

Fill the center of the aspic ring with the orange and onion salad, and arrange extra orange slices around the ring if you wish.

ORANGE AND ONION SALAD
2 tablespoons wine vinegar
½ teaspoon salt
Freshly ground black pepper
6 tablespoons olive oil
½ teaspoon lemon juice
4 navel oranges, peeled, and either thinly sliced or sectioned
2 red onions, peeled, thinly sliced and separated into rings

ORANGE AND ONION SALAD: In a large mixing bowl beat the wine vinegar, salt, a few grindings of black pepper, the olive oil and lemon juice with a wire whisk or fork until they are all well combined. Add the oranges and onions, and toss them together gently. Taste for seasoning.

Broiled Long Island Duckling

To serve 4

One 5- to 6-pound Long Island
duckling, cut into quarters

MARINADE

3/4 cup vegetable oil
1/2 cup red-wine vinegar
1 teaspoon salt
Freshly ground black pepper
1 cup thinly sliced onion
3 large garlic cloves, thinly sliced
2 large bay leaves, coarsely crumbled
Salt, preferably the coarse (kosher) variety

Wash the duck under cold running water and pat thoroughly dry. With poultry shears or a sharp knife, trim the quarters, cutting away all exposed fat. In a shallow glass, porcelain or stainless-steel pan large enough to hold the duck quarters in one layer, mix the oil, vinegar, salt and a few grindings of pepper. Add the onion, garlic and bay leaves. Lay the duck in this marinade, baste thoroughly and marinate at room temperature at least 3 hours, turning the pieces every half hour.

When you are ready to broil the duck, remove it from the marinade. Strain the marinade through a fine sieve and discard the vegetables. Preheat the broiler to its highest point. Arrange the duck, skin side down, on the broiler rack, sprinkle lightly with salt and broil 4 inches from the heat for about 35 minutes, regulating the heat or lowering the rack so the duck browns slowly without burning. Baste every 10 minutes or so with the marinade. Turn the pieces over with tongs, sprinkle with salt and broil 10 to 15 minutes longer, basting 2 or 3 times with the marinade. When the duck is tender and a deep golden brown, arrange it on a heated serving platter. Pour the pan drippings over it and serve at once.

Roast Rock Cornish Game Hens with Pine-Nut Stuffing

To serve 4

STUFFING
5 tablespoons butter
1 cup long-grain rice
2 cups chicken stock, fresh or canned
1 teaspoon salt
1 cup finely chopped onion
½ cup pine nuts
6 tablespoons finely chopped fresh parsley

4 Rock Cornish game hens, about 1 pound each
2 teaspoons salt
4 tablespoons melted butter
Watercress

For the stuffing, melt 3 tablespoons of the butter in a 2-quart heavy casserole or saucepan over moderate heat. Add the rice and stir constantly for 2 to 3 minutes, or until most of the rice has turned milky and opaque. Do not let it brown. Then pour in the chicken stock, add the salt and bring the stock to a boil, stirring occasionally. Cover the pan tightly, reduce the heat to its lowest point and simmer for 18 to 20 minutes, or until the rice has absorbed all the liquid. Meanwhile, in a small skillet melt the remaining 2 tablespoons of butter and when the foam subsides add the onion. Cook over moderate heat for 8 to 10 minutes, then add the pine nuts. Cook 2 or 3 minutes longer, stirring, until the nuts are lightly browned. In a small mixing bowl combine the cooked rice, the onion, pine nuts and the parsley. Mix gently but thoroughly. Taste for seasoning.

Preheat the oven to 400°. Wash the birds under cold running water, then dry them inside and out with paper towels. Sprinkle the inside of each bird with ½ teaspoon of salt, then pack the cavities loosely with the stuffing; they should be no more than ¾ full. Skewer or sew the openings with thread, truss the birds securely and brush them with the melted butter. Place them on their sides on a rack set in a shallow roasting pan just large enough to hold them. Roast them in the middle of the oven for 15 minutes, then turn them on the other side and brush them with butter again. Roast for another 15 minutes. Turn them breast side up, brush with the remaining butter and salt each bird lightly. Roast, basting occasionally with the drippings in the bottom of the pan, for 15 to 20 minutes longer, or until the birds are golden brown all over and tender. Test for doneness by piercing the fleshy part of the thigh with the point of a sharp knife. The juice that spurts out should be yellow. If it is pink, roast a few minutes longer. Transfer the birds to a warm serving platter, pour the pan juices over them and serve, garnished with watercress.

Roast Pheasant with Applejack Cream Sauce

To serve 4

STUFFING
4 tablespoons butter
¼ cup finely chopped onion
2 pheasant livers, coarsely chopped
1½ cups ½-inch-diced day-old bread
½ cup peeled, cored and diced apple, cut into ½-inch cubes
1 tablespoon parsley
Salt
Freshly ground black pepper

To make the stuffing, melt 2 tablespoons of the butter over moderate heat in an 8-inch skillet. When the foam subsides, add the chopped onion and the pheasant livers. Stirring frequently, cook the mixture for 3 to 4 minutes until the livers have stiffened slightly. Scrape the mixture into a bowl. Add the remaining 2 tablespoons of butter to the same skillet and, over high heat, brown the diced bread in it for 3 to 4 minutes. Add it to the livers in the mixing bowl. Mix in the apples and parsley, taste for seasoning, and add salt and pepper to taste.

2 drawn pheasants, approximately 1 pound each
2 tablespoons soft butter
4 strips bacon, cut in half
½ cup applejack
½ cup chicken stock, fresh or canned
¼ cup heavy cream

Preheat the oven to 375°. Wash the pheasants quickly under cold water and dry them thoroughly inside and out with paper towels. Rub the soft butter into the skins of each of them and fill their cavities with the stuffing. Do not pack it in too firmly. Secure the openings with skewers or sew with strong white thread. Truss the birds by tying their legs together with cord. Drape the bacon strips over their legs and breasts, and place them, breast side up, on a rack set in a shallow baking pan just large enough to hold the birds comfortably. Roast undisturbed in the center of the oven for about 30 minutes. Remove the pan from the oven and sprinkle the birds lightly with salt and pepper. Heat ¼ cup of the applejack in a small pan. Set it alight with a match and pour it flaming over the birds, shaking the pan gently until the flames die out. Baste thoroughly with the accumulated roasting-pan juices and return the pheasants to the oven. Roast for 10 to 12 minutes, or until the birds are brown, crisp and tender. Remove to a heated platter and make the sauce.

Pour the chicken stock and the remaining applejack into the roasting pan and bring it to a boil on the top of the stove, scraping into it any brown bits clinging to the bottom and sides of the pan. Boil briskly for 2 to 3 minutes, then stir in the cream. Bring to a boil once more, taste for seasoning, and either pour the sauce over the pheasants or serve it separately in a gravy boat.

Carve the pheasants by splitting them along their length into halves with a sharp carving knife or shears, allowing ½ bird per person.

Broiled Squab with Lemon-Soy Butter

To serve 4

4 squabs, about ¾ pound each
1 cup melted butter (½ pound)
2 tablespoons soy sauce
1 teaspoon lemon juice
Salt
Freshly ground black pepper
Watercress

Prepare the squabs for broiling by cutting them down the back from the neck to the tail with a large knife or poultry shears. Then spread the squabs out skin side up and, with a sharp blow of a meat cleaver or wooden mallet, break the curved rib bones so that the birds lie flat. Twist the wing tips under the shoulders.

Preheat the broiler to its highest point. Combine the butter, soy sauce and lemon juice in a large, shallow baking dish. Dip the squabs, one at a time, in the butter mixture to saturate them thoroughly. Arrange them, skin side down, on the broiler rack and sprinkle them generously with salt and a few grindings of black pepper. Slide the rack about 3 inches below the heat and broil the squabs for about 6 minutes undisturbed. Then brush them with the butter and turn them over with tongs. Brush the squabs with more of the butter mixture, sprinkle generously with salt and a few grindings of black pepper and broil about 6 minutes longer. Watch them carefully for any sign of burning and regulate the broiler heat accordingly. The squabs should be crisp and golden brown when they are done. To serve, arrange them on a heated platter and pour the broiler pan juices over them. Garnish with crisp watercress. The spoon bread on page 89 would make a fine accompaniment.

Roast Dove or Pigeon

To serve 4

- 4 doves or pigeons, approximately 1 pound each
- 4 tablespoons soft butter, unsalted
- ½ teaspoon thyme
- 2 teaspoons finely chopped fresh tarragon or ½ teaspoon dried tarragon
- 2 tablespoons finely chopped fresh parsley
- ½ teaspoon salt
- Freshly ground black pepper
- 2 small onions, peeled and halved
- 2 tablespoons butter
- 2 tablespoons oil
- 2 strips of bacon, cut in half
- 4 tablespoons finely chopped onion
- 2 cups chicken stock, fresh or canned
- 6 green olives, blanched and sliced

Wash the birds under cold running water and dry them thoroughly with paper towels inside and out. In a mixing bowl, cream the butter by beating it against the side of the bowl with a wooden spoon until it is light and fluffy. Then beat in the thyme, tarragon, parsley, ½ teaspoon salt and pepper. Rub the cavities of the birds with salt and then with the butter mixture, dividing it equally among them. Place ½ onion inside each bird and truss them securely.

Preheat the oven to 425°. In a heavy 12-inch skillet, heat the butter and oil over moderate heat. When the foam subsides add the birds to the skillet and brown them on all sides for about 10 minutes, turning them with tongs. Be careful not to let them burn. Then transfer them to a rack set in a shallow roasting pan that is just large enough to hold all of them comfortably.

Tie ½ strip of bacon on the breast of each bird and roast in the middle of the oven for 20 minutes. Reduce the heat to 350° and roast for 20 minutes more, basting the birds every 5 minutes or so with the drippings in the pan.

When they are done, remove the trussing strings, transfer the birds to a heated platter and sprinkle them lightly with salt. Cover the platter loosely with a piece of foil to keep the birds warm while you make the sauce. Add the chopped onions to the drippings remaining in the roasting pan and cook them over moderate heat on top of the stove for 2 to 3 minutes. Then pour in the chicken stock and bring to a boil, stirring in any brown bits clinging to the bottom and sides of the pan. Boil briskly until the sauce is reduced to about half its volume. Strain it into a saucepan. Skim the surface of as much fat as you can and stir in the sliced green olives. Cook for a minute or so until they are heated through, and serve in a gravy boat.

NOTE: To blanch the olives, cover them with cold water in a small saucepan and bring to a boil. Cook briskly for 2 minutes, or a few minutes longer if the olives seem excessively briny, then drain and run cold water over them.

Roast Quail on Toast

To serve 4

- 8 quail, about 1/4 pound each
- Salt
- Freshly ground black pepper
- 8 small, peeled white onions, about 1/2 inch in diameter
- 8 sprigs parsley
- 8 two-inch pieces of celery
- 4 strips bacon, cut in half
- 1/2 cup melted butter (1 quarter-pound stick)
- 1 cup chicken stock, fresh or canned
- 8 rounds of hot buttered toast, about 3 1/2 inches in diameter

Preheat the oven to 475°. Wash the quail quickly under cold running water and pat them thoroughly dry inside and out with paper towels. Sprinkle the cavities of the quail generously with salt and a few grindings of black pepper. Then stuff each of them with an onion, a sprig of parsley and a piece of celery. Truss the birds by tying their legs securely together, and place them side by side on a rack set in a shallow roasting pan just large enough to hold them comfortably. Drape each bird with a strip of bacon, then roast them in the middle of the oven for 15 to 20 minutes, basting every 5 minutes or so with liberal amounts of the melted butter. When the quail are a golden brown, cut away their trussing strings, and with a small spoon scoop out the cavity vegetables and discard them. Set the birds on individual rounds of toast arranged on a heated serving platter and keep them warm in the turned-off oven while you make the sauce.

Pour into the roasting pan the cup of chicken stock and bring it quickly to a boil, scraping into it any brown bits clinging to the bottom and sides of the pan. Continue to boil briskly until the stock is reduced to about half its volume, then, off the heat, stir into it any of the remaining basting butter. Taste for seasoning, pour a spoonful or so over each bird and serve at once.

Fried Pheasant with Cream Gravy

To serve 4 to 6

6 slices bacon
2 pheasants, cut into serving pieces
Salt
Freshly ground black pepper
½ cup flour
¼ cup finely chopped onion
2 tablespoons flour
1½ cups heavy cream

In a 10- or 12-inch heavy skillet, fry the bacon slices over moderate heat until they have rendered all their fat and are brown and crisp. Set them aside on paper towels to drain, and when cool break them into bits.

Wash the pieces of pheasant under cold running water and pat them thoroughly dry with paper towels. Then sprinkle them generously with salt and a few grindings of black pepper, and dip them in the flour. Shake each piece vigorously to remove any excess flour. Heat the bacon fat remaining in the skillet over high heat until a light haze forms above it. Fry the pheasant, skin side down, for about 5 minutes, regulating the heat so that the pieces brown evenly without burning. Turn them over with kitchen tongs and fry them 3 to 4 minutes longer. Now reduce the heat to low, cover the skillet tightly and cook the pheasant for about 20 minutes, or until it is tender, but don't overcook. Arrange the pieces attractively on a heated platter, and cover it loosely with a sheet of foil to keep the pheasant warm while you make the sauce.

Pour off all but a thin film of the fat from the skillet. Add the onion and cook over moderate heat for 3 to 4 minutes until soft but not brown. Remove from the heat and stir in the 2 tablespoons of flour. When it is completely absorbed and forms a thick paste, pour in the cream. Bring to a boil, beating with a whisk until the sauce thickens slightly. Stir in the reserved bacon bits, simmer a moment or two, and taste the sauce for seasoning; it will probably need some salt. Pour over the pheasant or serve separately in a heated gravy boat.

Fish and Shellfish

Dilled Salmon Soufflé

To serve 6

4 tablespoons butter
4 tablespoons finely chopped onion
4 tablespoons flour
1 cup milk
5 egg yolks
1 tablespoon tomato paste
1½ cups canned salmon, thoroughly drained and flaked (2 seven-ounce cans)
3 tablespoons finely cut fresh dill
1½ teaspoons lemon juice
1½ teaspoons salt
⅛ teaspoon cayenne
6 egg whites
Hollandaise sauce (optional)

Preheat the oven to 400°. Coat the bottom and sides of a 2-quart soufflé dish with a tablespoon of the butter and melt the remaining butter in a heavy saucepan. When the foam subsides add the onion and cook over moderate heat for about 3 minutes. Do not let the onions brown. Off the heat, mix in the flour and stir it to a smooth paste. Add the milk all at once and beat with a whisk to partially dissolve the flour. Then cook over moderate heat, whisking constantly, until the sauce is smooth and very thick. Remove the pan from the heat and beat into it, one at a time, the 5 egg yolks, then stir in the tomato paste, salmon, dill, lemon juice, salt and cayenne. Cool slightly. Meanwhile, with a large whisk or rotary beater, beat the egg whites, preferably in an unlined copper bowl, until they are stiff enough to form unwavering peaks on the beater when it is lifted out of the bowl. Stir a heaping tablespoon of the whites into the salmon mixture, then with a rubber spatula, fold in the remaining egg whites gently but thoroughly until no white streaks show; be careful not to overfold. Pour the mixture into the soufflé dish, reduce the heat to 375° and bake the soufflé undisturbed in the center of the oven for 35 to 40 minutes, or until it has puffed and is lightly brown on top. Serve, if you like, with the hollandaise sauce on page 81.

Baked Stuffed Striped Bass

To serve 4

STUFFING:

2 tablespoons butter
2 tablespoons finely chopped scallions, including part of the green stem
2 tablespoons finely chopped green pepper
1 medium tomato, peeled, seeded and coarsely chopped
1 tablespoon finely chopped parsley
Salt
Freshly ground black pepper

For the stuffing, melt the 2 tablespoons of butter in a small skillet over moderate heat. When the foam subsides, add the chopped scallions and green pepper and cook, stirring constantly, for 2 to 3 minutes until the vegetables are wilted but not brown. Scrape into a small mixing bowl. Add the chopped tomato, parsley, salt and a few grindings of black pepper. Mix thoroughly.

A 2½- to 3-pound striped bass, eviscerated but head and tail left on (or other firm white-meat fish such as red snapper, pompano, haddock, cod, pollack, rockfish, whitefish or lake trout)
4 tablespoons melted butter
1 medium onion, peeled and thinly sliced
1 small green pepper, seeded and thinly sliced
6 sprigs fresh dill
½ cup dry vermouth
1 tablespoon lemon juice
Salt
Freshly ground black pepper

Preheat the oven to 375°. Wash the fish inside and out under cold running water, and dry it thoroughly with paper towels. Fill the fish with the stuffing, sew the opening with thread or close it with small skewers and crisscross kitchen string around the skewers to secure them. Brush 2 tablespoons of the melted butter on the bottom of a shallow, flameproof baking dish attractive enough to serve from, and place the fish in it, surrounding it with the sliced onion, the green pepper and sprigs of fresh dill.

Combine the vermouth with the lemon juice and the rest of the melted butter, pour it over the fish and vegetables and bring it to a boil on top of the stove. Sprinkle the fish with salt and a few grindings of black pepper, and immediately transfer the baking dish to the middle of the oven. Bake uncovered for about 30 minutes, basting the fish every 8 minutes or so with the pan juices. The fish is done when it is firm to the touch and flakes easily when prodded gently with a fork. Serve directly from the baking dish.

Barbecued Swordfish

To serve 4 to 6

MARINADE

2 tablespoons lemon juice
4 tablespoons orange juice
4 tablespoons soy sauce
2 tablespoons tomato paste
1 teaspoon minced garlic
1 teaspoon oregano
2 tablespoons finely chopped fresh parsley
½ teaspoon salt
Freshly ground black pepper

2 pounds swordfish, cut about 1 inch thick
1 tablespoon soft butter

Combine the lemon and orange juice, soy sauce, tomato paste, garlic, oregano, parsley, salt and a few grindings of black pepper in a large, shallow baking dish. Stir until all the ingredients are well combined. Place the swordfish in the dish, baste thoroughly and marinate for about 2 hours at room temperature, turning the fish over after the first hour.

Preheat the broiler to its highest point for at least 10 minutes. Then, with a pastry brush, grease the broiler rack with the tablespoon of soft butter. Lay the swordfish on the rack, brush heavily with the marinade and broil the fish 3 inches from the heat for about 5 minutes, brushing it once or twice with the marinade. When the surface of the fish is lightly browned, turn it over with a large spatula and broil on the other side for 5 minutes, brushing on the remaining marinade once or twice more to keep the surface of the fish well moistened. When the swordfish is done it should be a golden brown and firm to the touch. Be careful not to overcook. Transfer the fish to a heated platter, pour the broiling pan juices over it and serve at once, cut into appropriate portions.

Pompano Stuffed with Shrimp and Crab en Papillote

To serve 6

6 pompano fillets, about 7 inches long and weighing in all about 2½ to 3 pounds
Salt
¾ cup thoroughly degreased chicken stock, fresh or canned
¼ cup dry white wine
2 tablespoons butter
2 tablespoons finely chopped shallots or scallions
3 tablespoons flour
2 tablespoons heavy cream
½ teaspoon lemon juice
½ teaspoon salt
⅛ teaspoon cayenne
6 teaspoons soft butter
1 cup coarsely diced cooked shrimp
1 cup coarsely diced crab meat, fresh or canned

Preheat the oven to 250°. Wash the fillets quickly in cold water and dry them on paper towels. Salt them lightly and arrange them folded in half end to end in a shallow, lightly buttered baking dish large enough to hold them in 1 layer. Pour in the chicken stock and white wine, and add a little water if the liquid doesn't come halfway up the sides of the fish. Heat the baking dish on top of the stove until the liquid begins to simmer.

Then cover the dish loosely with a sheet of wax paper, a little larger than the dish itself, and poach the fish in the middle of the oven for about 6 minutes, or until the fillets are opaque and almost, but not quite, cooked through. Remove the fish from the pan with a large metal spatula and spread them open on a platter.

Strain the poaching liquid through a fine sieve into a small saucepan and, over high heat, boil it rapidly uncovered until it is reduced to 1 cup. Set aside. In another saucepan, melt the 2 tablespoons of butter over moderate heat.

When the foam subsides, add the chopped shallots or scallions and, stirring constantly, cook them for 2 to 3 minutes until they are soft but not brown. Stir in the flour and cook for a moment or two until it froths, then pour in the cup of reserved poaching liquid. Cook over moderate heat, stirring constantly with a whisk until the sauce is smooth and thick. Add the 2 tablespoons of cream, the lemon juice, salt and cayenne. Taste for seasoning.

Cut 6 sheets of parchment cooking paper or aluminum foil into 12-by-14-inch heart shapes. Brush each heart with a teaspoon of soft butter. Fold each heart in half lengthwise, then open it and lay a fillet alongside the center crease of each heart.

Put an equal amount of the shrimp and crab meat on the lower half of each fillet and moisten it with a tablespoon of the sauce. Then fold the other half of the fish over it, enclosing the stuffing. Pour the remaining sauce over each fillet, dividing it equally. Seal the hearts securely by crimping and rolling the edges of the halves firmly together.

Preheat the oven to 450°. Place the *papillotes* side by side on a lightly greased cookie sheet and bake them in the middle of the oven for about 8 minutes. The parchment paper will puff and brown. Serve the *papillotes* on individual heated plates and cut them open at the table.

Brook Trout

To serve 4

8 strips of fat bacon
4 brook trout, about 3/4 to 1 pound each, eviscerated but with heads and tails left on
Salt
Freshly ground black pepper
1 1/2 to 2 cups white or yellow cornmeal

In a large, heavy skillet, cook the bacon over moderate heat until it has rendered all its fat and is brown and crisp. Transfer the bacon to paper towels to drain.

Wash the fish under cold running water and dry them thoroughly with paper towels. Sprinkle them inside and out with salt and a few grindings of black pepper, then dip them in the cornmeal, shaking them gently to remove any excess. Heat the bacon fat in the skillet over high heat until a light haze forms over it. Add the fish and cook them for about 5 minutes on each side, turning them over carefully with tongs. Regulate the heat so that the trout will brown evenly without burning. Remove them to a heated platter, arrange the bacon strips around them and serve at once.

Broiled Shad

To serve 4 to 6

6 tablespoons butter, cut into small pieces
2½ pounds shad, filleted but with skin left on
Salt
Freshly ground black pepper
Lemon wedges

Preheat the broiler to its highest point. Choose a shallow, flameproof baking dish just large enough to hold the shad fillets comfortably. In it, over moderate heat, melt the butter on top of the stove. Wash the shad quickly in cold water, pat thoroughly dry with paper towels and dip in the butter. Turn over 2 or 3 times so that the fish is thoroughly coated with butter on both sides. Broil the fish, skin side down, about 4 inches from the heat, for 6 to 8 minutes, regulating the heat, if necessary, to prevent the fish from burning. Baste occasionally with the butter in the pan. Do not turn the shad over. The shad is done when its flesh is opaque and flakes easily when gently prodded with a fork. Before serving, preferably in its baking dish, sprinkle the shad lightly with salt and a few grindings of black pepper, and surround with the lemon wedges.

Sautéed Shad Roe

To serve 4

2 pairs shad roe
Salt
Freshly ground black pepper
½ cup flour
8 tablespoons butter (1 quarter-pound stick), cut into small pieces
1 teaspoon Worcestershire sauce
2 teaspoons lemon juice
2 tablespoons finely cut chives
1 tablespoon finely chopped parsley
Cooked crisp bacon slices (optional)

With scissors or a small, sharp knife, slit the membranes connecting the shad roes. Sprinkle the roes with salt and a few grindings of black pepper, then dip them in the flour on both sides and shake off the excess. Over moderate heat, melt 6 tablespoons of the butter in a heavy 8-inch skillet. When the foam subsides add the roes and cook them for about 6 minutes on each side, regulating the heat so that the roes brown evenly and quickly without burning. Carefully transfer them to a heated platter and quickly make the sauce.

Stir the Worcestershire sauce, lemon juice, chives and parsley into the butter remaining in the skillet, add the remaining 2 tablespoons of butter and heat until the butter melts. Pour over the roes, and serve at once, accompanied by slices of crisp bacon if you like.

Fried Smelts with Herb Butter

To serve 4 to 6

8 tablespoons softened butter (1 quarter-pound stick)
1/2 teaspoon salt
Freshly ground black pepper
1 tablespoon finely chopped parsley
1 tablespoon finely chopped chives
1 tablespoon fresh lime juice
1/8 teaspoon Tabasco
18 smelts, with the backbone removed but the heads and tails left on
Salt
Flour
1 1/2 to 2 cups vegetable shortening

Cream the butter by beating it with a wooden spoon against the sides of a mixing bowl until it is smooth and fluffy. Beat in the 1/2 teaspoon of salt, a few grindings of black pepper, the parsley, chives, lime juice and Tabasco.

Place the herb butter on a sheet of wax paper about 3 feet long; fold the wax paper over it, and pat and shape the enclosed butter into a long, 1/2-inch-thick cylinder. Refrigerate it for at least an hour, or until the butter is firm.

Wash the smelts under cold running water and pat them thoroughly dry, inside and out, with paper towels. If the fish dealer has not removed the backbone, sever it from the head, and with the tip of a sharp knife gently lift it out, cutting it off at the base of the tail.

Sprinkle the fish generously with salt and a few grindings of pepper, dip it in flour on both sides and shake off the excess. Heat the shortening (it should be at least 1/2 inch deep in the pan) over high heat in a 10-inch heavy skillet until a light haze forms over it. Add as many of the fish, spread open, as the pan will hold comfortably, and cook them over moderate heat on both sides for 3 to 4 minutes each until they are crisp and brown. Remove them to a double thickness of paper towels to drain, and brown the remaining fish in the same fashion, adding more shortening to the pan if necessary.

Place the fish, spread open and skin side down, on a heated serving platter. Quickly, cut the chilled herb butter into approximately 1- to 2-inch lengths depending upon the size of the fish, and place a small cylinder, lengthwise, in the center of each fish. Serve at once before the butter has melted.

Palace Court Salad

To serve 6

1 pound medium-sized raw shrimp, shelled and deveined

Bring 1 quart of lightly salted water to a boil in an enameled or stainless-steel saucepan. Drop in the shrimp and boil them briskly for about 5 minutes, or until they turn pink and are firm to the touch. Do not overcook. Drain them at once and plunge them into cold water to stop their cooking. Drain again on paper towels and chill.

DRESSING

1¼ cups mayonnaise, freshly made, or a good, unsweetened commercial variety
¼ cup chili sauce, strained
1 tablespoon chopped fresh chives
2 tablespoons finely chopped fresh parsley
1 teaspoon fresh tarragon, finely chopped, or ½ teaspoon dried tarragon
Salt
White pepper

To make the dressing, in a small bowl combine the mayonnaise and the strained chili sauce, the chives, parsley and tarragon. Mix together thoroughly and taste. Season with salt and white pepper if necessary.

SALAD

1 teaspoon lemon juice
½ teaspoon salt
3 tablespoons mayonnaise
2 cups shredded iceberg lettuce
6 half-inch slices tomato, about 2½ inches in diameter
6 artichoke bottoms, canned or freshly cooked
3 hard-cooked eggs, finely chopped
6 strips pimiento (optional)

For the shrimp mixture, toss all but 6 of the shrimp (reserve them for the garnish) with the lemon juice and ½ teaspoon salt. Then add 3 tablespoons of mayonnaise to the shrimp and stir gently until they are well coated.

Construct the salad on individual chilled salad plates. Place a thin bed of shredded lettuce about 3 to 4 inches in diameter in the center of each plate. Put a tomato slice in the center of the lettuce, arrange an artichoke bottom on top of it and spoon equal amounts of the shrimp mixture into the slight hollow of each artichoke bottom. Sprinkle the chopped egg around the exposed circle of lettuce and garnish each mound of shrimp with the reserved shrimp. Top with a strip of pimiento if desired. Serve chilled and pass the dressing separately.

NOTE: This salad is often made with Dungeness crab and decorated with crab legs. Any crab meat may be substituted for the shrimp.

Shrimp Mousse

To serve 4

2 teaspoons vegetable oil
½ cup chicken stock, fresh or canned, and thoroughly degreased
¼ cup dry white wine
1 pound raw shrimp, shelled and deveined
1 envelope unflavored gelatin
¼ cup cold water
¼ cup finely chopped onion
1 tablespoon fresh tarragon or 1 teaspoon dried tarragon
1 tablespoon tomato paste
1 tablespoon lemon juice
1 teaspoon salt
Pinch of white pepper
1 cup heavy cream, chilled
1 cup freshly made mayonnaise *(page 80)* or a good unsweetened commercial variety (optional)

Brush a 1½-quart decorative mold, preferably a fish mold, with the 2 teaspoons of oil and then invert it on a paper towel and let the excess oil drain off.

Bring the chicken stock and wine to a boil in a small enameled or stainless-steel saucepan, and drop in the shrimp. Boil rapidly, uncovered, for 3 to 4 minutes, or until the shrimp turn pink and are firm to the touch. Remove them with a slotted spoon to a bowl. Soften the gelatin in the ¼ cup of cold water for 5 minutes, then stir it into the stock and simmer over low heat for a minute or two, stirring constantly, until the gelatin has completely dissolved. Cool to lukewarm. Cut the shrimp into ¼-inch pieces and combine it with the stock, the chopped onion and tarragon in the container of an electric blender. Blend at high speed until the mixture is a smooth purée. Then scrape it into a mixing bowl and stir in the tomato paste, lemon juice, salt and pepper. Taste for seasoning.

With a whisk or rotary or electric beater, whip the cream only to the point when it holds soft peaks on the beater when it is lifted out of the bowl. Set the bowl of puréed shrimp into a larger bowl filled with ice and stir it with a rubber spatula until it begins to thicken slightly. Immediately fold in the whipped cream, continuing to fold until streaks of white no longer show. Pour the mousse into the mold, smooth the top with a spatula and refrigerate for at least 2 hours until firm.

To unmold the mousse, run a small knife around the inside edge of the mold and dip the bottom of the mold briefly in hot water. Place a chilled platter on top of it, invert it and rap it once or twice on the table. The mousse should slide out easily. Serve with mayonnaise if desired.

Jambalaya

To serve 4 to 6

- 1/4 pound sliced bacon, cut in 1-inch pieces
- 1/2 cup finely chopped onion
- 2 medium-sized green peppers, seeded and cut in 1-inch strips
- 1 cup raw rice
- 1 teaspoon finely chopped garlic
- A 1-pound 3-ounce can whole-pack tomatoes, drained and coarsely chopped
- 1/2 teaspoon thyme
- 1 teaspoon salt
- Freshly ground black pepper
- 1 1/2 to 2 cups chicken stock, fresh or canned
- 1/2-pound cooked smoked ham, cut in 2-inch by 1/2-inch strips
- 1 pound medium-sized raw shrimp, shelled and deveined
- 1 tablespoon finely chopped fresh parsley

Preheat the oven to 350°. In a heavy 3- or 4-quart casserole, fry the bacon over moderate heat until it has rendered its fat and is brown but not crisp. Drain on paper towels and reserve. Add the onions to the fat in the pan and cook them for 8 to 10 minutes, stirring occasionally until they are transparent but not brown. Mix in the green peppers. They will wilt slightly in about 3 minutes, at which point the rice should be stirred in. Turn the rice about in the hot fat and vegetables over moderate heat until the grains become somewhat opaque and milky. Then add the garlic, tomatoes, the bacon, thyme, salt and a few grindings of black pepper, stirring them together thoroughly. Pour in 1 1/2 cups of chicken stock and bring it to a boil. Add the ham and stir again. Cover the casserole tightly and place it in the lower third of the oven. After 10 minutes add the shrimp, pushing them down beneath the rice, and continue to cook tightly covered for about 10 minutes longer, or until all of the stock is absorbed and the rice is tender. If at any point during this time the rice appears dry, add a few tablespoons more of the hot stock to it. Serve directly from the casserole if you wish, or mound the jambalaya on a large, heated platter. Garnish with fresh chopped parsley.

Barbecued Shrimp

To serve 4 to 6

2 pounds fresh shrimp, 16 or 18 to the pound

MARINADE

1 cup olive oil
2 tablespoons red-wine vinegar
1 tablespoon tomato paste
1 tablespoon oregano
1 teaspoon minced garlic
3 tablespoons finely chopped fresh parsley
1 teaspoon salt
Freshly ground black pepper

Shell each shrimp carefully by breaking off the shell just above the point where it joins the tail, but don't remove the tail. With a small knife, make a shallow incision down the back of the shrimp and lift out the intestinal vein. Wash the shrimp thoroughly in cold water and pat them dry with paper towels. In a large mixing bowl combine the olive oil, vinegar, tomato paste, oregano, garlic, parsley, salt and a few grindings of black pepper. Drop in the shrimp, mix and turn them about in the marinade until they are well coated. Marinate at room temperature for about 2 hours, stirring gently every ½ hour or so.

Preheat the broiler to its highest point. Pour the shrimp and all its marinade into a shallow, ovenproof baking dish and spread the shrimp out in one layer. Slide the baking dish onto the broiler rack set about 3 inches from the heat. Broil for about 5 minutes, basting the shrimp with the marinade at the end of 3 minutes. Then turn them over with tongs and broil for 3 to 5 minutes longer, or until the shrimp are lightly browned and the flesh firm to the touch. Be careful not to overcook. Serve the barbecued shrimp either directly from the baking dish or in a large serving platter with a well deep enough to hold the sauce. The shrimp are customarily eaten by holding one by the tail and dipping it into the sauce. Hot French or Italian bread for dunking is almost a must with this.

Artichokes Stuffed with Shrimp and Green Goddess Dressing

To serve 6

Six 10- to 12-ounce artichokes

6 quarts water
3 tablespoons salt

Trim the bases of the artichokes flush and flat so that they will stand upright without wobbling. Bend and snap off the small bottom leaves and any bruised outer leaves. Lay each artichoke on its side, grip it firmly and, with a large, sharp knife, slice about 1 inch off the top.

With scissors trim 1/4 inch off the points of the rest of the leaves. Rub all the cut edges with lemon to prevent their discoloring. In an 8-quart enameled or stainless-steel pot (do not use aluminum; it will turn the artichokes gray), bring about 6 quarts of water and 3 tablespoons of salt to a boil. Drop in the artichokes and boil them briskly, uncovered, for about 30 minutes, turning occasionally. They are done when their bases show no resistance when pierced with the tip of a small, sharp knife. Drain them upside down in a colander. When they are cool enough to handle, spread their leaves apart gently, grasp the inner core of yellow, thistlelike leaves firmly and ease it out. Then, with a long-handled spoon, thoroughly scrape out and discard the fuzzy choke.

GREEN GODDESS DRESSING

3 cups mayonnaise, freshly made, or a good, unsweetened commercial variety
1 tablespoon tarragon wine vinegar
1 teaspoon lemon juice
1 tablespoon finely chopped anchovies (6 to 8 flat anchovies canned in olive oil)
1 tablespoon chopped fresh tarragon or 1 teaspoon dried crumbled tarragon
1/4 cup finely chopped scallions, including part of the green stems
1/4 teaspoon finely chopped garlic
1/4 cup finely chopped parsley
1/8 teaspoon cayenne

GREEN GODDESS DRESSING: In a small mixing bowl, beat into the 3 cups of mayonnaise the vinegar, lemon juice, anchovies, tarragon, scallions, garlic, parsley and cayenne. Taste for seasoning and add a little salt if you think it needs it.

2 pounds shelled, cooked and chilled tiny shrimp, preferably the West Coast or Alaskan variety
6 rolled, caper-stuffed anchovies (optional)
Lemon slices

In a large mixing bowl combine the shrimp and 1½ cups of the dressing, stirring them gently until the shrimp are well coated. Fill each artichoke cavity with the mixture, mounding it slightly on the top. Arrange the anchovy, if you are using it, in the center of each shrimp mound and chill the stuffed artichokes until ready to serve.

To serve, place the artichokes on chilled plates and surround them with the lemon slices. Pass the remaining Green Goddess dressing separately.

Deviled Crab

To serve 4

- 1/2 cup finely chopped celery
- 1/3 cup finely chopped green pepper
- 1/2 cup thinly sliced scallions, including about an inch of the green stems
- 1/4 cup finely chopped parsley
- 1 pound lump crab meat, freshly cooked, or the canned variety, thoroughly drained
- 1 3/4 cups coarsely crushed soda crackers
- 1/2 teaspoon salt
- 1/2 teaspoon dry mustard
- Tabasco
- 1/4 cup heavy cream
- 3/4 cup melted butter

Preheat the oven to 350°. In a large mixing bowl, combine the celery, green pepper, scallions, parsley, crab meat (with all cartilage removed), 1 1/2 cups of the crushed crackers, salt, mustard, a few drops of Tabasco, the cream and 1/2 cup of the melted butter. Mix together gently but thoroughly with a large spoon and taste for seasoning.

Spoon the mixture into a buttered 1 1/2-quart casserole and sprinkle the remaining cracker crumbs evenly over the top. Dribble over it the remaining butter and bake the casserole in the upper third of the oven for about 1/2 hour, or until the crumbs are golden brown. Serve at once, directly from the casserole.

Cioppino

To serve 6

½ cup vegetable oil
1 cup finely chopped onion
1 medium green pepper, seeded and coarsely chopped
2 teaspoons finely chopped garlic
4 medium-sized tomatoes, peeled, seeded and coarsely chopped, or an equivalent amount of canned tomatoes, thoroughly drained
2 tablespoons tomato paste
2 cups dry white wine
½ cup finely chopped fresh parsley, Italian flat-leaf if possible
1 teaspoon salt
Freshly ground black pepper
2 live lobsters, about 1¼ pounds each, cut into serving pieces, or 1 large Dungeness crab, or 4 small blue crabs
2½ to 3 pounds firm white-fleshed fish, cut into serving pieces
1 pound raw, medium-sized shrimp, shelled and deveined
1½ dozen small hard-shelled clams in their shells, well washed and scrubbed
1½ dozen small mussels in their shells, well washed, scrubbed and bearded

In a heavy 6- to 8-quart casserole, heat the oil over high heat until a light haze forms above it. Then add the chopped onions, green pepper and garlic, and cook, stirring occasionally, for 4 to 6 minutes, or until the vegetables are wilted but not brown. Add the tomatoes, tomato paste, wine, ¼ cup of the chopped parsley, salt and a few grindings of pepper, and bring to a boil. Lower the heat, half cover the casserole and simmer the sauce for about 15 minutes.

Add the lobster or crab, baste thoroughly with the sauce and cook over low heat, tightly covered, for about 10 minutes before adding the cut-up fish. Cover the casserole again and cook the fish for about 8 minutes, or until it is firm to the touch. Add the shrimp, pushing them beneath the sauce and cook for 3 to 4 minutes, or until they turn pink and are firm.

Meanwhile, steam open the clams and mussels by dropping them into a large skillet or casserole filled with about 1 inch of boiling water. Cover the pan tightly and cook the shellfish over moderate heat for 5 to 10 minutes, or until their shells open. Steam those that do not open a little longer, finally discarding any that remain closed. Add the opened mussels and clams (shells and all) to the casserole and baste thoroughly with the sauce. If you like, strain the broth from the steamed shellfish through cheesecloth and add it to the cioppino. However, be careful not to thin the sauce too much.

Cover the pan and cook the cioppino about 2 to 3 minutes longer, then taste for seasoning. Serve either directly from the casserole or from a large tureen. In either case, sprinkle with the remaining ¼ cup of chopped parsley and accompany the cioppino with hot garlic bread.

Frogs' Legs, Roadhouse Style, with Tartar Sauce

To serve 4

24 pairs baby frogs' legs (if frozen, thoroughly defrosted)
2 cups milk
½ teaspoon salt
4 tablespoons paprika
1½ cups flour
Vegetable oil or shortening for deep frying

Gently split the frogs' legs apart and wash them under cold running water. Pat them thoroughly dry with paper towels. In a small bowl, mix together the milk, salt and 2 tablespoons of the paprika, and soak the frogs' legs in the mixture for about 5 minutes. Combine the flour and the remaining paprika, and place on a sheet of wax paper.

In a heavy 12-inch skillet, heat the oil (which should be about 2 inches deep) over high heat until a light haze forms above it. Dip the frogs' legs in the flour, shake loose any excess and fry them in the hot oil for about 5 minutes, turning them frequently with tongs. Regulate the heat so the legs brown quickly without burning. When they are golden brown, arrange them on paper towels to drain. Serve hot with tartar sauce.

TARTAR SAUCE

To make 1 cup

1 cup freshly made mayonnaise *(page 80)* or a good, unsweetened commercial variety
2 tablespoons finely chopped onion
1 tablespoon lemon juice
¼ cup finely chopped fresh dill
2 tablespoons finely chopped fresh parsley
Salt
Freshly ground black pepper

To make the sauce, combine the mayonnaise, finely chopped onion, lemon juice, dill and parsley. Taste for seasoning, and add as much salt and pepper as you think it needs.

Clam Hash

To serve 4 to 6

6 slices bacon
4 tablespoons butter
3/4 cup finely chopped onion
2 cups freshly shucked and minced clams, or canned minced clams, drained
3 cups coarsely diced, cooked, cold potatoes
2 tablespoons finely chopped parsley
1/2 teaspoon salt
Freshly ground black pepper

In an 8- or 10-inch heavy skillet, preferably of the nonstick variety, fry the bacon slices over moderate heat until they have rendered all their fat and are brown and crisp. Set them aside on paper towels to drain, and when cool break them into bits.

Pour off and reserve all the bacon fat and, in its place, add the butter. Melt it over moderate heat. When the foam subsides, add the onion and cook for 6 to 8 minutes, stirring occasionally, until soft but not brown. Scrape into a large mixing bowl and add the drained clams, potatoes, parsley, salt and a few grindings of black pepper. Mix together gently but thoroughly and taste for seasoning.

Pour 4 tablespoons of the reserved bacon fat into the skillet and set over moderate heat. Add the clam mixture and pat it down into the pan with a metal spatula. Cook for 10 to 15 minutes, shaking the pan back and forth every now and then to make sure the hash doesn't stick. When the bottom of the hash is golden brown, place a heated platter on top of the frying pan, and, grasping pan and platter firmly together, invert them and turn the hash out. Or, if you prefer, fold it like an omelet and slide it onto the platter. In either case, before serving, sprinkle the hash with the reserved bacon bits.

Scallops Remoulade

To serve 4 to 6

1½ to 2 pounds fresh bay scallops

Only very fresh, tiny bay scallops can be served raw successfully. (Frozen and defrosted ones will not do.) Wash the scallops quickly under cold running water and dry them thoroughly with paper towels. Chill until ready to serve.

REMOULADE SAUCE

1 cup mayonnaise, freshly made *(page 80)*, or a good unsweetened commercial variety
1 teaspoon dry mustard
1 teaspoon lemon juice
¼ to ½ teaspoon garlic, finely chopped
1 tablespoon capers, drained, washed and finely chopped
1 tablespoon fresh tarragon, finely chopped, or 2 teaspoons finely crumbled dried tarragon
1 tablespoon finely chopped parsley
1 hard-cooked egg, finely chopped
Salt
Cayenne or Tabasco

For the remoulade sauce, combine the mayonnaise, dry mustard and lemon juice in a small mixing bowl. Stir in the chopped garlic, capers, tarragon, parsley and hard-cooked egg. Mix together gently but thoroughly, and season to taste with salt and a few grains of cayenne pepper or drops of Tabasco. Arrange the scallops, pierced with decorative picks, on a chilled serving plate and pass the remoulade sauce separately.

Lobster Newburg

To serve 4 to 6

6 tablespoons butter
3 cups cooked lobster, fresh or canned, cut into 2-inch pieces
1/3 cup Madeira or dry sherry
1 1/2 cups heavy cream
5 egg yolks
3/4 teaspoon salt
1/8 teaspoon cayenne
1/2 teaspoon lemon juice
6 patty shells, or 2 to 3 cups of steamed rice, or 8 to 12 buttered toast points
Paprika (optional)

In a large enameled or stainless-steel skillet, melt the butter over moderate heat. When the foam subsides, add the lobster meat and, stirring constantly, cook for about a minute. Pour in the Madeira or sherry and 1 cup of the heavy cream and, stirring, bring it to a boil. Reduce the heat to its lowest point and, still stirring, cook for about 2 minutes. In a small bowl, beat the egg yolks into the remaining 1/2 cup of cream. Beat into them 4 tablespoons of the simmering lobster sauce, and then, in a slow stream, pour the mixture back into the skillet, stirring constantly. Cook over moderate heat until the sauce thickens, but under no circumstances let it come to a boil or it will curdle. Season with the salt, cayenne and lemon juice. Serve immediately in patty shells, on beds of steamed rice, or on hot buttered toast points, and sprinkle the lobster Newburg lightly with paprika if you like.

Scalloped Clams

To serve 4 to 6

1 1/2 cups freshly shucked and minced clams, or canned minced clams, drained
4 tablespoons finely chopped onion
3 tablespoons finely chopped parsley
1 teaspoon Worcestershire sauce
1/2 cup melted butter (1 quarter-pound stick)
Salt
Freshly ground black pepper
1 cup coarsely crushed soda crackers
3/4 cup fresh bread crumbs
1/2 cup heavy cream
2 tablespoons soft butter, cut into small bits

Preheat the oven to 375°. In a large mixing bowl, combine the clams, onion, parsley, Worcestershire sauce, melted butter, salt and a few grindings of black pepper. Stir in the crushed soda crackers and 1/2 cup of the fresh bread crumbs, pour in the cream and mix together gently but thoroughly. Taste for seasoning. Transfer the mixture to a lightly buttered 1-quart casserole and sprinkle the remaining bread crumbs over the top.

Dot with the 2 tablespoons of butter and bake in the center of the oven for about 25 minutes, or until the crumbs are lightly brown. For a crisper, browner crust you may, if you like, slide the casserole under a preheated broiler for 30 seconds or so. Serve as a first course or luncheon dish directly from the casserole.

Pacific Oyster Stew

To serve 4

- 4 tablespoons soft butter
- 1½ pints light or heavy cream
- 1½ pints Pacific oysters, or other oysters, and their liquor
- Salt
- Freshly ground black pepper
- Paprika (optional)

Warm 4 deep soup bowls in a shallow baking pan that is half filled with boiling water. Add 1 tablespoon of soft butter to each bowl. In a small saucepan, bring the cream almost but not quite to a boil over moderate heat. When small bubbles appear around the edge of the pan, reduce the heat to its lowest point and keep the cream barely simmering.

Pour the oysters and all their liquor into a 12-inch enameled or stainless-steel skillet. Set it over moderate heat and poach the oysters, turning them gently about in their liquor with a wooden spoon for 2 or 3 minutes, or until the oysters plump up and their edges begin to curl. Immediately pour the simmering cream into the skillet, add salt and pepper to taste, and simmer a moment longer. Ladle the stew into heated soup bowls, sprinkle with a little paprika if you like and serve at once accompanied by crackers or, less traditionally, hot French or Italian bread.

Oyster Fritters

To serve 4 to 6

1 cup flour
½ teaspoon salt
1 tablespoon melted butter
1 egg, lightly beaten
½ cup beer
2 dozen fresh oysters, shucked, or 2 dozen frozen oysters, thoroughly defrosted
1 egg white
Vegetable shortening or vegetable oil for deep-fat frying
Lemon wedges

Sift ½ cup of the flour and the salt into a mixing bowl. With a wooden spoon stir in the butter and the egg. Then pour in the beer gradually and mix only until the batter is fairly smooth. Don't overmix. Let the batter rest at room temperature for about an hour. When you are ready to fry the oysters, beat the egg white with a rotary beater or whisk until it is stiff enough to form unwavering peaks on the beater when it is lifted out of the bowl. Gently fold the beaten egg white into the batter and continue to fold until no streaks of white remain.

In a deep-fat fryer, heat the shortening or oil until it registers 375° on a deep-frying thermometer. The fat should be at least 3 inches deep. Dip the oysters in the remaining ½ cup of flour, shake off any excess and then dip in the batter. Let the excess batter drain off, then fry the oysters, 5 or 6 at a time, for 3 to 4 minutes until they are puffed and golden brown. Drain on paper towels and keep the fritters warm in a 200° oven until all the oysters have been fried. Serve at once with wedges of lemon.

Eggs and Cheese

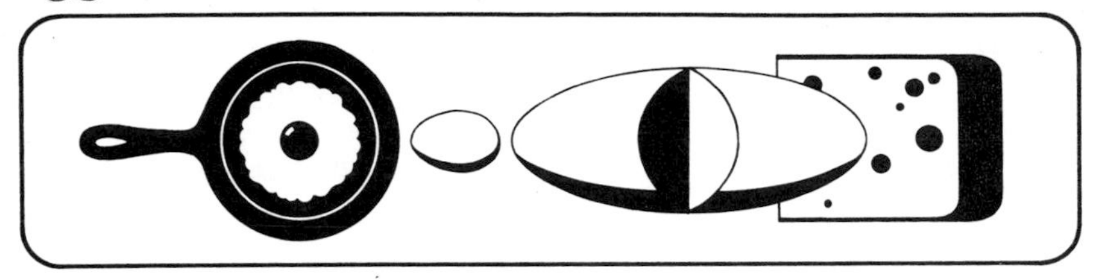

Grits and Cheddar Cheese Casserole

To serve 4 to 6

2 tablespoons butter
1/4 cup finely chopped onion
2 cups water
1/2 teaspoon salt
1/2 cup quick grits
1 teaspoon Tabasco
Freshly ground black pepper
1 3/4 cups grated Cheddar cheese
3 tablespoons soft butter
2 egg whites

In a small skillet, melt 2 tablespoons of butter over moderate heat. When the foam subsides add the 1/4 cup of onion and cook for 4 or 5 minutes until translucent but not brown. Meanwhile, bring the 2 cups of water to a bubbling boil in a 1-quart saucepan. Add the salt and pour in the grits slowly without allowing the water to stop boiling. Boil for about a minute, stirring constantly, then reduce the heat to medium and cook for another 2 minutes. With a rubber spatula, scrape into the saucepan the onions and add the Tabasco, a few grindings of black pepper and 1 1/2 cups of the grated Cheddar cheese combined with the 3 tablespoons of soft butter.

Preheat the oven to 400°. Lightly butter a 1-quart casserole or soufflé dish. With a wire whisk or rotary beater, beat the egg whites until they form stiff peaks on the beater when it is lifted from the bowl. With a rubber spatula, thoroughly fold the egg whites into the grits mixture. Pour into the casserole and sprinkle the top with the remaining grated Cheddar cheese. Bake in the middle of the oven for about 30 minutes, or until the mixture has puffed and browned. Serve at once as an accompaniment for any meat or poultry dish.

Blender Mayonnaise

To make approximately 1 cup

1 egg
1/4 teaspoon dry mustard
1/2 teaspoon salt
2 teaspoons lemon juice or wine vinegar
2/3 cup vegetable oil, or equal amounts of vegetable and olive oil

Combine the whole egg, mustard and salt in the container of an electric blender. Cover the jar and blend at top speed for 30 seconds. Pour in the lemon juice or wine vinegar and, still blending at high speed, pour in the oil as slowly as possible. If the mayonnaise thickens too much at any point, add a few more drops of lemon juice or vinegar.

Macaroni, Ham and Cheese Casserole

To serve 4 to 6

3 quarts water
1 tablespoon salt
2 cups elbow macaroni
4 tablespoons butter
4 tablespoons flour
2 cups milk
1 teaspoon salt
1/8 teaspoon cayenne
2 cups cooked ham, cut into 1/4-inch dice
1 3/4 cups grated sharp Cheddar cheese
1 tablespoon grated onion
2 tablespoons dry bread crumbs
2 tablespoons melted butter

In a 4- to 5-quart pot, bring the water and the salt to a boil over high heat. Pour the macaroni in slowly so that the water never stops boiling. Cook briskly, uncovered, for about 20 minutes, or until the macaroni is tender. Then drain it thoroughly in a colander.

Melt the butter over moderate heat in a small saucepan. Add the flour and cook, stirring until the mixture froths and foams. Add the milk all at once and stir with a wire whisk until the sauce thickens into a smooth cream. Add the salt and cayenne, and simmer over very low heat for about 2 minutes. Pour the sauce into a large mixing bowl, and stir in the macaroni, diced ham, 1 1/2 cups of the cheese and the grated onion. Taste for seasoning.

Preheat the oven to 375°. Lightly butter a 2 1/2- or 3-quart casserole. Spoon in the macaroni mixture and spread the bread crumbs, mixed with the remaining cheese and melted butter, evenly over the top. Bake in the middle of the oven for 30 to 40 minutes, or until the cheese and bread crumb topping is lightly brown. Serve directly from the casserole.

Eggs Benedict

To serve 2 to 4

4 eggs
6 cups water
1 tablespoon white vinegar
4 three-inch rounds of white bread, 1/2 inch thick, or 2 English muffins
4 teaspoons soft butter
Four 1/4-inch-thick slices cooked ham, cut into rounds 3 inches in diameter

To poach eggs successfully they must be very fresh or the whites will come away from their yolks during the poaching process. Pour 6 cups of water into a 10-inch enameled or stainless-steel skillet. Add 1 tablespoon of white vinegar and, over high heat, bring the water to a boil. Reduce the heat to low and, when the water is barely simmering, gently drop the eggs in one at a time, carefully turning the whites over the yolks with a wooden spoon. Let the eggs poach undisturbed for 3 to 4 minutes, or until the whites are set and the yolks still fluid. Remove them with a slotted spoon and keep them warm in a bowl of warm water.

Preheat the oven to 250°. Toast the rounds of bread or the split English muffins, spread each half with about a teaspoon of soft butter and top with a slice of hot or cold ham. Arrange them on a heatproof serving platter or individual plates and keep them warm in the oven while you make the hollandaise sauce.

BLENDER HOLLANDAISE

1/4-pound stick of butter, cut into 1/2-inch pieces
3 egg yolks
1 teaspoon lemon juice
1/4 teaspoon salt
Pinch of white pepper

BLENDER HOLLANDAISE: Melt the butter without browning it and keep it warm over very low heat. Combine the egg yolks, lemon juice, salt and pepper in the container of an electric blender. Cover the jar and blend at high speed for about 2 seconds. Then remove the cover and, still blending at high speed, slowly pour in the hot butter. For a finer sauce do not pour in the whey or milky solids on the bottom of the pan, although it will not be disastrous if you do. Taste for seasoning.

Working quickly, remove the poached eggs from the bowl of water and drain them on a kitchen towel. Place an egg atop each slice of ham, pour hollandaise sauce over each of them and serve at once.

Chiles Rellenos

To serve 4

- 8 fresh green chili peppers, peeled and seeded, or 2 four-ounce cans of roasted and peeled chilis
- 1 pound Monterey Jack cheese, cut into 1-inch cubes
- 4 egg whites
- 4 egg yolks
- ½ teaspoon salt
- ¼ cup flour
- Vegetable shortening for deep frying

To prepare the fresh chilis, preheat the oven to 475°. Place the chilis side by side on a rack in a shallow roasting pan and bake them for 8 to 10 minutes until their skins scorch and blacken slightly. Remove from the oven and wrap them in a damp, clean towel. Let them rest in the towel a few minutes, then gently rub with the towel until the skins slip off. Cut the chilis in half lengthwise and remove the seeds. Canned chilis need only be drained of their canning liquid and any seeds discarded. Handle them gently; they disintegrate easily. Carefully wrap a strip of chili around each cube of cheese, enclosing it completely. Skewer with toothpicks.

For the batter, first beat the egg whites in a mixing bowl with a whisk or rotary beater until they form firm, unwavering peaks when the beater is lifted out of the bowl. Without washing the beater, in a separate bowl beat the egg yolks for 2 or 3 minutes until they are thick and lemon colored. Then beat in the salt and the flour. With a rubber spatula, gently fold the beaten egg whites into this mixture. Heat the vegetable shortening in a deep fryer (the fat should be at least 3 inches deep) until it reaches a temperature of 375° on a deep-fat-frying thermometer. (The chilis may also be fried in a skillet containing 2 inches of hot oil, lard or vegetable shortening. If you choose this method, turn them over with a large spoon to brown them on all sides.) Dip the chilis in the batter and when they are well coated drop them into the hot fat. Turn them gently in the fat with a large spoon, and cook them until they puff and turn a golden brown on all sides. Drain on paper towels and serve.

Breads, Rolls and Breakfast Cakes

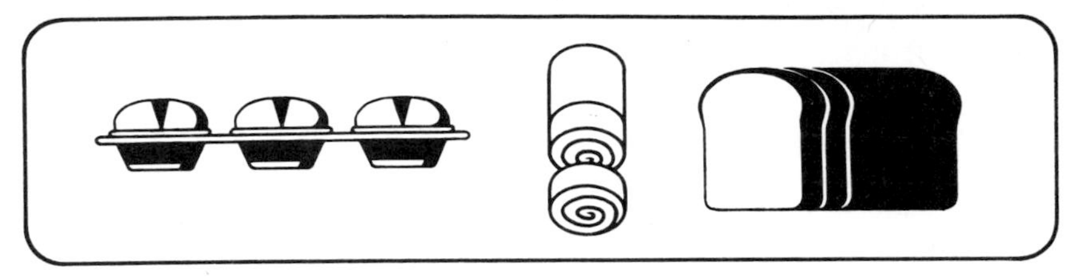

Snipdoodle

To make one 12-inch cake

1 cup vegetable shortening
1⅓ cups sugar
2 eggs
2⅔ cups flour
4 teaspoons baking powder
½ teaspoon salt
1⅓ cups milk
¼ cup sugar combined with 1 teaspoon cinnamon

Preheat the oven to 350°. In a large mixing bowl, cream the vegetable shortening and the sugar by mashing and beating them together with a large spoon. When the mixture is light and fluffy, beat in the eggs, one at a time, thoroughly incorporating one before adding the other. Sift the flour, baking powder and salt together into another bowl, and beat ¼ cup of this into the egg mixture. Then beat in ¼ cup of the milk. Continue adding the flour and milk alternately in similar amounts, beating until the batter is smooth.

Lightly butter and flour an 8-by-12-inch shallow baking pan. Invert the pan and rap it on the edge of the table to knock out any excess flour. Pour in the batter and bake in the middle of the oven for 45 minutes, or until the cake comes slightly away from the edge of the pan and is firm to the touch. As a further test, a toothpick inserted in the center should come out dry and clean.

Sprinkle the top of the cake evenly with the cinnamon-sugar and cut the cake into 2-inch squares. With a metal spatula, transfer them from the pan to a cake plate and serve warm or at room temperature for breakfast or for tea.

American White Bread

To make one 9-inch loaf

2 packages or cakes dry or compressed yeast
1 cup lukewarm milk
1½ tablespoons sugar
4 cups all-purpose flour or bread flour
4 tablespoons soft butter
1 tablespoon salt

GLAZE

1 egg, lightly beaten with 1 tablespoon milk

Sprinkle the yeast into a half cup of the lukewarm (110° to 115°) milk. Add 1 teaspoon of the sugar and stir until thoroughly dissolved. Place the mixture in a warm, draft-free place—such as an unlighted oven—for 5 to 8 minutes, or until the yeast has begun to bubble and almost doubled in volume.

Then pour it into a large mixing bowl, add the remaining ½ cup of milk and stir until the yeast is dissolved. With a large spoon, slowly beat into the mixture 1 cup of the flour and continue to beat vigorously until smooth. Still beating, add the butter, remaining sugar, salt and 2 more cups of flour. Transfer the dough to a lightly floured surface and knead it by folding it end to end, then pressing it down, pushing it forward and folding it back for at least 10 minutes, sprinkling the dough every few minutes with small handfuls of as much of the remaining flour as you need to prevent the dough from sticking to the board. When the dough is smooth and elastic, place it in a large, lightly buttered bowl. Dust it with a sprinkling of flour and cover the bowl loosely with a kitchen towel. Let the dough rise in a warm, draft-free place for 45 minutes to an hour, or until the dough doubles its bulk and springs back slowly when gently poked with a finger. Then punch the dough down again with one blow of your fist to reduce it to its original volume. Let it rise 30 to 40 minutes until it again doubles in bulk.

Preheat the oven to 425°. Lightly but thoroughly butter a 9-by-5-by-3-inch loaf pan. Shape the dough into a compact loaf, somewhat high and round in the center, and place it in the pan. Cover with a towel and let the dough rise in the same warm place (about 25 minutes) until it reaches the top of the pan. Thoroughly brush the top of the loaf with the egg and milk glaze. Bake in the lower third of the oven for 30 to 40 minutes, or until the loaf is golden brown and a toothpick inserted in its center comes out clean and dry. Invert the bread on to a cake rack and cool before slicing.

Clover Leaf Rolls

To make 24 rolls

1 recipe for American white-bread dough *(opposite)*
1 tablespoon soft butter
2 tablespoons melted butter

Prepare the dough as described in the white-bread recipe above up to the point where it has risen for the second time. With a pastry brush, lightly but thoroughly grease each cup of two 12-cup muffin tins with 1 tablespoon of soft butter. Pinch off small pieces of the dough and shape them into small balls, rolling them between your palms until they are about ½ inch in diameter. Arrange 3 balls closely together in each muffin cup, cover the tins with a dry kitchen towel and let the dough rise in a warm place (about 25 minutes) until each roll reaches the top of the pan.

Preheat the oven to 425°. Brush the dough with the melted butter and bake in the middle of the oven for 10 to 15 minutes until the rolls are golden brown. Test for doneness by inserting a toothpick in a roll; it should come out dry and clean. Remove the rolls from the tins and serve them while they are still hot and crusty.

Baking Powder Biscuits

To make 16

3 cups all-purpose flour
2 tablespoons baking powder
1½ teaspoons salt
1 cup vegetable shortening
1 cup milk
3 tablespoons melted butter

Preheat the oven to 400°. Sift the flour, baking powder and salt together in a large mixing bowl. Add the shortening, and, with your fingers, rub the flour and fat together until the mixture is well combined and resembles coarse meal. Make a well in the center and pour in the milk. Mix together only long enough to form a soft dough. Knead it for about 30 seconds on a lightly floured board, then roll it into a circle about ½ inch thick. Cut the dough into 2-inch rounds with a cookie cutter. Gather together any remaining scraps of dough, roll out again and cut into more rounds. Brush a cookie sheet with enough of the melted butter to coat it lightly, arrange the biscuits side by side on it and brush each biscuit with the remaining butter. Bake in the middle of the oven for about 20 minutes, or until the biscuits are a delicate golden brown. Serve hot.

Sticky Buns

To make 12 buns

2 packages or cakes of dry or compressed yeast
Pinch sugar
½ cup lukewarm water (110° to 115°)
1 cup milk
8 tablespoons melted butter (1 quarter-pound stick)
½ cup sugar
3½ cups all-purpose flour
¼ teaspoon salt
2 egg yolks
1 teaspoon grated lemon rind
1 teaspoon cinnamon
½ cup currants or raisins
½ cup water
1½ cups brown sugar, packed down
4 tablespoons butter
½ cup coarsely chopped walnuts

Sprinkle the yeast and a pinch of sugar into the lukewarm water. Let the mixture stand for 2 to 3 minutes, then stir it to dissolve the yeast. Set the container in a warm, draft-free place, such as an unlighted oven, for 5 to 8 minutes, or until the solution has begun to bubble and has almost doubled in volume.

Pour the milk into a heavy 1-quart saucepan and warm it over medium heat until bubbles form around the edge of the pan. Turn the heat to low and add 4 tablespoons of the butter and ¼ cup of the sugar. Stir constantly until the sugar dissolves, then cool to lukewarm and combine with the yeast mixture.

Sift the flour and salt into a deep mixing bowl. Make a well in the flour and pour into it the yeast and milk mixture, the egg yolks and the teaspoon of lemon rind. With your hands or a large wooden spoon, work the flour into the other ingredients until they become a medium-firm dough.

On a lightly floured surface, knead the dough by folding it end to end, then pressing it down and pushing it forward several times with the heel of your hand. Sprinkle the dough with a little extra flour whenever necessary to prevent it from sticking to the board. Repeat the kneading process until the dough becomes smooth and elastic. This will take about 10 minutes.

Shape the dough into a ball and put it in a large, lightly buttered bowl. Dust the top of the dough lightly with flour, cover with a kitchen towel and set in a warm, draft-free spot (again, an unlighted oven is ideal). In 45 minutes to an hour, the dough should double in bulk.

Punch the dough down with your fist, then transfer from the bowl to a lightly floured board and knead again briefly. Roll it out into a rectangle 12 inches long and ¼ inch thick. Brush the dough with 3 tablespoons of the remaining melted butter and sprinkle the combined ¼ cup of sugar, the cinnamon and currants or raisins over it evenly.

In a small, heavy saucepan, combine the ½ cup of water, the brown sugar and 4 tablespoons of butter. Stir until the sugar dissolves and bring to a boil over high heat. Reduce the heat to moderate and cook the syrup for about 10 minutes until it has the consistency and color of maple syrup.

Let the syrup cool slightly, then dribble half of it over the surface of the dough. With your hands, roll the dough into a tight cylinder about 2 inches in diameter and cut it crosswise into 1-inch rounds. Grease a round 10-inch cake pan with the remaining 1 tablespoon of melted butter. Pour into it the other half of the syrup and sprinkle it evenly with the chopped walnuts. Arrange the rounds, cut side down, in a circle around the edge of the pan; continue the pattern with the remaining rounds until the pan is full. Let them rise in a warm, draft-free place for about 25 minutes, or until they are double in bulk. Meanwhile, preheat the oven to 350°.

Bake the buns in the middle of the oven for about 1/2 hour. When the buns are golden brown and firm to the touch, remove them from the oven and invert them onto a cake rack. Separate the buns and serve warm or at room temperature.

Leola's Cornbread

To make one 9-inch loaf

1 1/2 cups yellow cornmeal
1 cup all-purpose flour
1/3 cup sugar
1 teaspoon salt
1 tablespoon baking powder
2 eggs
6 tablespoons melted and cooled butter
8 tablespoons melted and cooled vegetable shortening
1 1/2 cups milk

Preheat the oven to 400°. Sift into a mixing bowl the cornmeal, flour, sugar, salt and baking powder. Beat the eggs lightly, add the melted butter and shortening, and stir in the 1 1/2 cups of milk. Pour into the bowl of dry ingredients and beat together for about a minute, or until smooth. Do not overbeat. Lightly butter a 9-by-5-by-3-inch loaf pan or 8-by-12-inch shallow baking pan and pour in the batter. Bake in the center of the oven for about 30 minutes, or until the bread comes slightly away from the edge of the pan and is golden brown. Serve hot.

Griddle Cakes

To make 18 to 20 pancakes

2 cups all-purpose flour
2 teaspoons baking powder
2 teaspoons sugar
1 teaspoon salt
3 eggs, lightly beaten
2 cups milk
1/4 cup melted butter
1/4 cup vegetable oil

Sift the flour, baking powder, sugar and salt together into a large mixing bowl. Make a well in the center of the flour and pour into it the eggs and milk. With a large spoon mix together only long enough to blend, then stir in the melted butter. Do not overmix; the pancakes will be lighter if the batter is not too smooth. Heat a griddle or heavy skillet over moderate heat until a drop of water flicked onto it evaporates instantly. Grease the griddle or skillet very lightly with a pastry brush dipped in oil; continue to grease when necessary. Pour the batter from a pitcher or small ladle into the hot pan to form pancakes 4 inches in diameter. Cook 2 to 3 minutes until small, scattered bubbles have formed—but have not broken—on the surface . Immediately turn with a spatula and cook for a minute until the other side of the pancake is golden brown. Stack on a heated plate and serve with melted butter and maple syrup.

NOTE: One cup of thoroughly drained, fresh, canned or thoroughly defrosted and drained frozen fruit may be added to the batter before frying.

Popovers

To make 8

2 eggs
1 cup milk
1 cup all-purpose flour
1/4 teaspoon salt
2 tablespoons melted vegetable shortening

Preheat the oven to 450°. In a large mixing bowl, beat the eggs with a rotary or electric beater for a few seconds until they froth. Still beating, pour in the milk, and then the flour, salt and a tablespoon of the melted shortening. Continue to beat until the mixture is smooth, but don't overbeat.

With a pastry brush, grease an 8-cup muffin tin or, preferably, heavy popover pans, with the remaining shortening. Pour enough batter into each cup to fill it about 2/3 of the way to the top. Bake in the center of the oven for 20 minutes. Then reduce the heat to 350° and bake 10 to 15 minutes longer, or until the popovers have puffed to their fullest height, and are golden brown and crusty. Serve at once.

NOTE: The popover batter may more easily be made in a blender if you have one. Simply combine all the ingredients in the blender container and whirl at high speed for 30 to 40 seconds, stopping the machine and scraping down the sides of the jar after the first 10 seconds. Bake as described above.

Spoon Bread

To serve 4 to 6

1 cup milk
½ cup yellow cornmeal
½ teaspoon salt
3 tablespoons butter
3 egg yolks
3 egg whites

Preheat the oven to 375°. Over moderate heat, in a 2-quart saucepan, heat the milk until small bubbles form around the side of the pan. Slowly pour in the cornmeal, stirring constantly, and cook without boiling until the mixture is thick and smooth. Add the salt and butter, and stir until the butter has been completely absorbed. Then remove from the heat. Add the egg yolks to the mixture one at a time, beating vigorously after each addition. Lightly butter a 6-by-8-by-2-inch baking dish. With a whisk or rotary beater, beat the egg whites in a large bowl until they form unwavering peaks on the beater when it is lifted out of the bowl. Mix a large spoonful of the whites into the cornmeal mixture, then, with a rubber spatula, gently but thoroughly fold in the rest. Pour into the baking dish, smooth the top with a spatula and bake the spoon bread in the center of the oven for 35 to 40 minutes, or until golden brown. Serve directly from the baking dish with a large serving spoon.

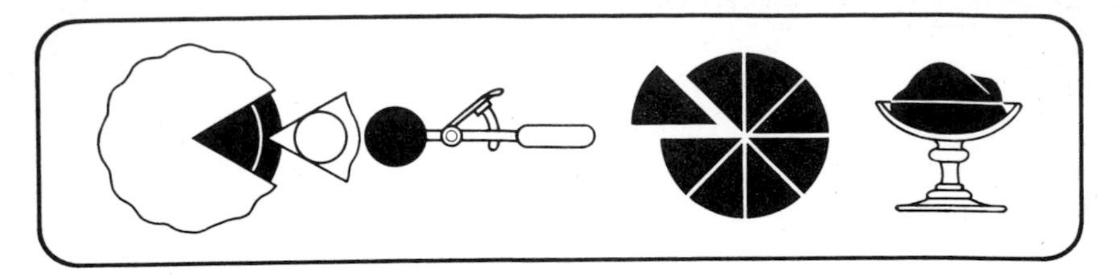

Strawberry Shortcake

To make 6 small shortcakes

4 cups all-purpose flour
6 tablespoons sugar
5 teaspoons baking powder
2 teaspoons salt
12 tablespoons butter (1½ quarter-pound sticks) chilled and cut into bits
1½ cups heavy cream
6 teaspoons melted and cooled butter
2 pints of fresh, ripe strawberries
1½ teaspoons sugar
1 pint heavy cream for topping

Preheat the oven to 450°. Sift the flour, sugar, baking powder and salt together into a large mixing bowl. Add the butter, and, with your fingertips, rub the dry ingredients and butter together until most of the lumps disappear and the mixture resembles coarse meal. Pour in the heavy cream and, with your hands or a large spoon, mix thoroughly until a soft dough is formed. Gather it into a compact ball and transfer it to a lightly floured board. Knead the dough for about a minute by folding it end to end and pressing it down and pushing it forward several times with the heel of your hand. Then roll the dough out into a circle about 1 inch thick. With a 3-inch cookie cutter, cut out 6 circles. Cut the remaining dough into six 2½-inch circles. (If there isn't enough dough, gather the scraps together, knead briefly and roll out again.) Arrange the 3-inch circles on a lightly buttered cookie sheet. Brush each with a teaspoon of melted butter, then top with the smaller circle. Bake in the middle of the oven for 12 to 15 minutes until firm to the touch and golden brown.

Meanwhile, chop half the strawberries coarsely, reserving the most attractive ones for the top. Separate the shortcakes. Spread a layer of chopped strawberries on the bottom circles, sprinkle with sugar and gently place the smaller circles on top. Garnish with the whole strawberries. Strawberry shortcake is traditionally served with heavy cream.

Three-Layer Chocolate Cake

To make one 9-inch cake

Six 1-ounce squares of unsweetened chocolate
12 tablespoons unsalted butter (1½ quarter-pound sticks), softened
2¼ cups sugar
4 eggs
1 teaspoon vanilla
2 cups all-purpose flour
1½ level teaspoons baking powder
¼ teaspoon salt
1½ cups milk

Preheat the oven to 375°. Break the chocolate into small pieces, place in a small saucepan and melt over moderate heat, stirring constantly with a spoon. Do not let it boil. Cool to room temperature. In a large mixing bowl, cream the butter and sugar together by mashing and beating it with a large spoon until it is light and fluffy. Beat in the eggs, one at a time, then beat in the melted chocolate and vanilla. Sift the flour, baking powder and salt together into another bowl. Beat ¼ cup of the dry ingredients into the chocolate mixture, then beat in ¼ cup of milk. Continue adding the flour and milk alternately in similar amounts, beating until the batter is smooth.

Butter and flour three 9½-inch circular cake pans. Invert the pans and rap them on the edge of the table to knock out any excess flour. Divide the batter equally among the three pans and bake them in the center of the oven for 15 to 20 minutes, or until the cakes come slightly away from the edge of the pan and are firm to the touch. A knife inserted in the center of the cakes should come out dry and clean. Turn the cakes out on cake racks to cool.

Spread the top of each cake with about ¼ inch of the chocolate sour-cream frosting and place the layers one on top of another on a cake plate. With a long metal spatula or knife, thoroughly coat the sides of the cakes with the remaining frosting, and add more frosting to the top of the cake if you wish. Decorate the top with the halved walnuts.

CHOCOLATE SOUR-CREAM FROSTING
Three 7-ounce packages semisweet chocolate bits
¼ teaspoon salt
1½ cups sour cream
12 to 15 shelled walnut halves

CHOCOLATE SOUR-CREAM FROSTING: In the top of a double boiler, melt the chocolate over boiling water. With a whisk or spoon, stir into it the salt and the sour cream. Ice the cake while the frosting is still slightly warm.

Orange-Walnut Torte

To make one 8-inch cake

1 tablespoon butter, softened
1/2 cup dry bread crumbs
6 egg yolks
10 tablespoons sugar
1/4 cup grated raw apple
Grated rind of 1 orange (about 2 tablespoons)
1 tablespoon lemon juice
1 tablespoon brandy
1/4 teaspoon salt
1 1/2 cups finely grated walnuts
6 egg whites
1 cup heavy cream, stiffly whipped

Preheat the oven to 325°. With a pastry brush, butter the bottom and sides of an 8-inch, 3-inch-deep springform cake pan. Toss in 1/4 cup of the bread crumbs and tip the pan from side to side to coat it evenly. Rap the pan sharply to dislodge any excess crumbs. With a whisk or rotary or electric beater, beat the egg yolks for about a minute, then slowly pour in 8 tablespoons of the sugar. Continue beating until the mixture falls back upon itself in a ribbon when the beater is lifted out of the bowl. Beat in the apple, orange rind, lemon juice, brandy and salt, and with a spatula fold in the remaining bread crumbs and walnuts. In another bowl beat the whites until they froth, then add 2 tablespoons of the sugar, continuing to beat until the whites form firm, unwavering peaks on the beater when it is lifted out of the bowl. Gently but thoroughly fold the whites into the egg yolk mixture until no streaks of white show. Pour the batter into the springform pan and with the spatula spread the mixture out evenly. Bake the torte in the center of the oven for 30 minutes, or until it has puffed and has begun to come slightly away from the sides of the pan. Turn off the heat and let the cake rest for 15 minutes before removing it from the oven. Remove the sides of the pan and cool the torte on a cake rack. With a spatula, spread the top of the cake with the whipped cream and serve.

Cherry Cobbler

To serve 6

- 1 cup all-purpose flour
- 2 tablespoons sugar
- 1½ teaspoons baking powder
- ½ teaspoon salt
- 2 tablespoons butter, chilled and cut into bits
- ⅔ cup heavy cream
- 2 tablespoons melted and cooled butter
- ½ cup sugar
- 2 one-pound cans pitted sour cherries, thoroughly drained, ¼ cup of juice reserved, or 2 pounds freshly cooked pitted cherries, with ¼ of their cooking liquid reserved
- 1 tablespoon arrowroot

Preheat the oven to 425°. Sift the flour, 2 tablespoons of sugar, baking powder and salt together into a large mixing bowl. Add the chilled butter, and, with your fingertips, rub the dry ingredients and butter together until most of the lumps have disappeared and the mixture resembles coarse meal. Pour in the heavy cream and mix thoroughly until a soft dough is formed. Gather it into a compact ball and transfer it to a lightly floured board. Knead the dough for about a minute by folding it end to end and then pressing it down and pushing it forward several times with the heel of your hand. Now roll the dough out into a circle about ½ inch thick. With a 2½-inch cookie cutter, cut out 6 circles and set them aside. In a large mixing bowl, combine 1 tablespoon of the melted butter, sugar, the ¼ cup of cherry juice and arrowroot, and stir together until the arrowroot has dissolved. Add the cherries, stir again, then pour the entire contents of the bowl into a 6-by-8-by-2½-inch ovenproof baking dish. Spread the cherries out in the dish and arrange the circles of dough over them side by side. Brush the dough with the remaining 1 tablespoon of melted butter. Bake in the middle of the oven for 25 to 30 minutes, or until the biscuits are a golden brown. Serve warm or at room temperature directly from the dish.

Cheesecake

To make one 9-inch cheesecake

1 six-ounce box Graham crackers, finely crumbled (3/4 cup)
2 tablespoons sugar
1/2 teaspoon cinnamon
6 tablespoons unsalted butter, melted
2 tablespoons soft butter

In a mixing bowl, with a large spoon combine the finely crumbled Graham crackers, the sugar and cinnamon. Stir the melted butter into the cracker crumbs until they are well saturated. With a pastry brush, heavily butter a 9-inch, 3-inch-deep springform pan with the 2 tablespoons of soft butter. With your fingers, pat an even layer of the cracker-crumb mixture on the bottom and sides of the pan to form a shell. Refrigerate while you make the filling.

FILLING
3 eight-ounce packages cream cheese, softened
1 1/4 cups sugar
6 egg yolks
1 pint sour cream
3 tablespoons all-purpose flour
2 teaspoons vanilla
1 tablespoon lemon juice
1 tablespoon finely grated lemon rind
6 egg whites
2 tablespoons confectioners' sugar

Preheat the oven to 350°. Cream the softened cheese by beating it with a spoon in a mixing bowl until it is smooth. Then gradually beat in the sugar. Beat in the egg yolks one at a time, and continue to beat until all the ingredients are well combined. Stir in the sour cream, flour, vanilla, lemon juice and lemon rind.

With a large whisk or rotary beater, beat the egg whites, preferably in an unlined copper bowl, until they are stiff enough to form unwavering peaks on the beater when it is lifted out of the bowl. With a rubber spatula fold the egg whites gently but thoroughly into the cream cheese mixture until no streaks of white show, but be careful not to overfold.

Pour the filling into the pan, spreading it out evenly with a rubber spatula. Bake in the middle of the oven for 1 hour. Then turn off the oven, and with the oven door open, let the cake rest on the oven shelf for 15 minutes. Remove and let cool to room temperature. Before serving, remove the sides of the pan and sprinkle the cake with confectioners' sugar.

Deep-Dish Peach Pie with Cream-Cheese Crust

To serve 6

8 tablespoons butter (1 quarter-pound stick), softened
8 tablespoons cream cheese, softened
1¼ cups all-purpose flour
2 tablespoons sugar
¼ teaspoon salt
2 tablespoons heavy cream

In a large mixing bowl, cream the butter and cheese by beating them together with a large spoon until smooth and fluffy. Sift the combined flour, sugar and salt into the mixture, add the cream and, with your hands or a large spoon, mix thoroughly until the dough can be gathered into a compact ball. Dust lightly with flour, wrap in wax paper and refrigerate while you prepare the filling.

FILLING
1½ pounds fresh peaches (8 to 10 medium-sized peaches)
1 tablespoon flour
2 tablespoons brown sugar
3 tablespoons melted butter
2 teaspoons vanilla
1 egg yolk, lightly beaten with 2 teaspoons cold water
1 teaspoon sugar

Preheat the oven to 350°. To peel the peaches easily, drop them into a pan of boiling water. Scoop them out after about 30 seconds, and while they are still warm, remove their skins with a small, sharp knife. Cut the peaches in half, discard the pits and slice thinly.

Combine the peaches, flour, brown sugar, melted butter and vanilla in a large bowl, and with a large spoon mix them together gently but thoroughly. With a rubber spatula, scrape the entire contents of the bowl into an 8-inch-square baking dish about 2½ inches deep. Spread the peaches out evenly. On a lightly floured surface, roll the pastry into a 10- to 11-inch square. Lift it up on the rolling pin and gently drape it over the top of the dish. Crimp the edges of the pastry to secure it around the outside of the dish and brush the pastry evenly with the egg-yolk-water mixture, then sprinkle with the sugar. Cut 2 small slits in the top of the pie to allow steam to escape and bake in the middle of the oven for 35 to 40 minutes, or until the crust is golden brown. Serve directly from the dish.

Apple Pie

To make one 9-inch pie

2½ cups all-purpose flour
8 tablespoons chilled vegetable shortening or lard
4 tablespoons chilled butter, cut in ¼-inch pieces
¼ teaspoon salt
6 tablespoons ice water
1 tablespoon melted and cooled butter

In a large mixing bowl, combine the flour, vegetable shortening or lard, butter and salt. Working quickly, use your fingertips to rub the flour and fat together until they look like flakes of coarse meal. Pour the ice water over the mixture, toss together, and press and knead gently with your hands until the dough can be gathered into a compact ball. Dust very lightly with flour, wrap in wax paper and chill for at least ½ hour.

Lightly butter a 9-inch pie plate and divide the ball of dough in half. On a floured surface, roll out half of the ball into a circle about ⅛ inch thick and 13 to 14 inches in diameter. Lift it up on the rolling pin and unroll it over the pie plate. Be sure to leave enough slack in the middle of the pastry to enable you to line the plate without pulling or stretching the dough. Trim the excess pastry with a sharp knife, so that the pastry is even with the outer rim of the pie plate. Preheat the oven to 375°.

FILLING
¾ cup granulated sugar
1 teaspoon cinnamon
¼ teaspoon allspice
¼ teaspoon nutmeg
1 tablespoon flour
6 cups of peeled, cored and sliced Greening apples, about ⅛-inch thick (1¾ to 2 pounds)
1 tablespoon lemon juice
2 tablespoons butter, cut in small pieces

For the filling, combine the sugar, cinnamon, allspice, nutmeg and flour in a large mixing bowl. Add the apples and the lemon juice, and toss together gently but thoroughly. Fill the pie shell with the apple mixture, mounding it somewhat higher in the center. Although the apple filling may appear quite high, it will shrink considerably during the baking. Dot the top of the filling with the 2 tablespoons of butter.

For the upper crust, roll out the remaining half of the dough into a circle the same size and thickness as the bottom crust. Lift it up on the rolling pin and drape it gently over the filling. With a scissors, trim the top crust to within ¼ inch of the pie plate. Tuck the overhanging ¼ inch under the edge of the bottom crust all around the rim and then press down with the tines of a fork to seal the two crusts securely. Brush the pastry evenly with the melted butter and cut two small gashes in the center of the top crust to allow the steam to escape. Bake the pie in the middle of the oven for 40 minutes, or until the crust is golden brown. Serve warm or at room temperature with vanilla ice cream or heavy cream.

Pumpkin Pie

To make one 9-inch pie

1¼ cups all-purpose flour
4 tablespoons chilled vegetable shortening or lard
2 tablespoons chilled butter, cut in ¼-inch pieces
⅛ teaspoon salt
3 tablespoons ice water

In a large mixing bowl, combine the flour, vegetable shortening or lard, butter and salt. Use your fingertips to rub the flour and fat together until they look like flakes of coarse meal. Pour the ice water over the mixture, toss together, and press and knead gently with your hands, only until the dough can be gathered into a compact ball. Dust very lightly with flour, wrap in wax paper and chill for at least ½ hour.

Lightly butter a 9-inch pie plate. On a floured surface, roll the dough out into a circle about ⅛ inch thick and 13 to 14 inches in diameter. Lift it up on the rolling pin and unroll it over the pie plate, leaving enough slack in the middle of the pastry to enable you to line the plate without pulling or stretching the dough. Trim the excess pastry with a sharp knife to within ½ inch of the pie plate and fold the extra ½ inch under to make a double thickness all around the rim of the plate. With the tines of a fork or with your fingers, press the pastry down around the rim. Preheat the oven to 350°.

FILLING

½ cup heavy cream
½ cup milk
¾ cup dark brown sugar
1 teaspoon cinnamon
⅛ teaspoon ground cloves
½ teaspoon ground ginger
3 eggs, lightly beaten
2 tablespoons applejack
1½ cups puréed pumpkin, freshly cooked or canned

In a large mixing bowl, combine the cream, milk, brown sugar, cinnamon, cloves and ginger. Stir thoroughly, then add the lightly beaten eggs and the applejack. Stir in the 1½ cups of puréed pumpkin. Carefully pour the filling into the pie shell. Bake for 40 to 50 minutes in the center of the oven until the filling is firm and the center of the pie barely quivers when the pie pan is gently moved back and forth. Serve warm or at room temperature with vanilla ice cream or stiffly whipped cream.

Banana Cream Pie

To make one 9-inch pie

PASTRY

1 1/4 cups all-purpose flour
4 tablespoons chilled vegetable shortening or lard
2 tablespoons chilled butter, cut in 1/4 inch pieces
1/8 teaspoon salt
3 tablespoons ice water

In a large mixing bowl, combine the flour, vegetable shortening or lard, butter and salt. Working quickly, use your fingertips to rub the flour and fat together until they look like flakes of coarse meal. Pour 3 tablespoons of ice water over the mixture, toss together, and press and knead gently with your hands until the dough can be gathered into a compact ball. Dust very lightly with flour, wrap in wax paper and chill the dough for at least 1/2 hour.

Lightly butter a 9-inch pie plate. On a floured surface, roll the dough out into a circle about 1/8 inch thick and 13 to 14 inches in diameter. Lift it up on the rolling pin and unroll it over the pie plate, leaving enough slack in the middle of the pastry to enable you to line the plate without pulling or stretching the dough. Trim the excess pastry with a sharp knife to within 1/2 inch of the pie plate and fold the extra 1/2 inch to make a double thickness all around the rim of the plate. With the tines of a fork or your fingers, press the pastry down around the rim.

Preheat the oven to 400°. To prevent the unfilled pastry from buckling as it bakes, either set another pie plate, lightly buttered on the underside, into the pastry shell, or line it with a sheet of lightly buttered foil. In either case, do not prick the pastry or the filling will run out when it is added later.

Bake the shell in the center of the oven for 10 minutes, remove the pie plate or foil, then turn the oven down to 350° for 10 minutes more, or until the pastry has lightly browned. Let the shell cool while you make the filling.

FILLING

1/2 cup granulated sugar
5 tablespoons flour
1/4 teaspoon salt
3 egg yolks
2 cups milk
2 tablespoons butter, cut into 1/2 inch pieces
1/2 teaspoon vanilla
2 tablespoons dark rum
1 1/2 cups chilled heavy cream
3 large, ripe bananas, peeled and sliced into 1/4-inch rounds

Sift the sugar, flour and salt into a large mixing bowl. With a large spoon, beat in the egg yolks one at a time. Heat the milk and 2 tablespoons of butter in a small saucepan until the butter melts and small bubbles form around the edge of the pan. Slowly, pour it into the mixing bowl, stirring constantly with a whisk. Add the vanilla and rum, and return the mixture to the saucepan. Bring almost to a boil, reduce the heat to low and simmer, stirring until it thickens to a smooth, heavy custard. Let it cool to lukewarm. Meanwhile, beat ½ cup of the cream with a whisk or rotary or electric beater until it forms firm peaks on the beater when it is lifted out of the bowl. With a rubber spatula, gently but thoroughly fold it into the custard. Spread ¼ inch of custard on the bottom of the pie shell and arrange a layer of bananas on top of it. Continue alternating a layer of custard with one of bananas, ending with a top layer of bananas. Beat the remaining cream until stiff, and either pipe it on top of the pie through a pastry bag fitted with a plain or decorative tip or spread it on with a spatula in decorative swirls. Chill for at least an hour before serving.

Lemon Pie

To make one 9-inch pie

1 fully baked 9-inch pastry shell *(see banana cream pie, opposite)*
7 egg yolks
¾ cup sugar
¼ cup lemon juice (1 to 2 medium-sized lemons)
1 teaspoon grated lemon rind
7 egg whites at room temperature
1 tablespoon confectioners' sugar

Preheat the oven to 350°. With a whisk or rotary or electric beater, beat the egg yolks for 30 seconds or so, then slowly pour in ½ cup of the sugar. Beat until the mixture is thick and falls back on itself in a ribbon when the beater is lifted out of the bowl. Stir in the lemon juice and lemon rind, and transfer the mixture to a small enameled or stainless-steel saucepan. Stirring constantly, cook over low heat for about 5 minutes, or until the mixture lightly coats a spoon. Under no circumstances must it boil or the eggs will curdle. Cool slightly.

Meanwhile, beat the egg whites, preferably in an unlined copper bowl, until they froth. Slowly pour in the remaining sugar and continue to beat until the whites form stiff, unwavering peaks on the beater when it is lifted out of the bowl. With a rubber spatula, mix about a third of the whites into the egg yolk mixture, then gently but thoroughly fold in the rest. With the rubber spatula, fill the pie shell, shaping the filling into swirls and mounding the peaks highest in the center. Bake in the center of the oven until the filling has firmed and lightly browned. Cool to room temperature and, before serving, dust with the confectioners' sugar.

Black Bottom Pie

To make one 9-inch pie

- 1 fully baked 9-inch pastry shell *(see banana cream pie, page 98)*
- 3 ounces semisweet chocolate, broken into small bits
- 4 egg yolks
- 4 teaspoons cornstarch
- ½ cup sugar
- 1½ cups milk
- ½ cup heavy cream
- 2 tablespoons dark rum
- ½ teaspoon vanilla
- 2 teaspoons unflavored gelatin
- 3 tablespoons cold water
- 2 egg whites
- 1 tablespoon sugar
- 1 cup chilled heavy cream
- 2 tablespoons confectioners' sugar
- 1 tablespoon thinly shaved semisweet chocolate

Over moderate heat, melt the chocolate in a small, heavy saucepan, stirring it constantly with a wooden spoon. Be careful not to let it boil. Set aside and cool to lukewarm. Meanwhile, in a large mixing bowl, beat the egg yolks and cornstarch with a whisk or rotary or electric beater for a minute or two, then add the sugar and continue beating until the mixture is pale yellow and falls back on itself in a ribbon when the beater is lifted out of the bowl. Heat the milk and ½ cup cream in a small saucepan until small bubbles form around the edge of the pan. Slowly pour it into the egg yolk mixture, stirring constantly with a whisk. Add the rum and vanilla, and return the mixture to the saucepan. Bring it almost to a boil, reduce the heat to low and simmer, stirring, until it thickens to a smooth custard. Mix 1½ cups of the custard into the lukewarm chocolate and when the mixture has cooled to room temperature, pour it into the baked pastry shell. Refrigerate it while you prepare the remaining filling.

In a measuring cup, soften the gelatin in 3 tablespoons of cold water for about 5 minutes, then set the cup in a pan of simmering water, and stir the gelatin until it dissolves and clears. Mix it into the remaining custard. With a whisk or electric or rotary beater, beat the egg whites and the tablespoon of sugar until they form firm unwavering peaks on the beater when it is lifted out of the bowl. With a rubber spatula, gently but thoroughly fold it into the custard. Then spread it evenly over the chocolate mixture in the pie shell and refrigerate for at least 2 hours, or until firm. Just before serving, beat the cup of cream until it holds soft peaks, then add 2 tablespoons of confectioners' sugar and beat until the cream is stiff. Pipe it on top of the pie through a pastry bag fitted with a plain or decorative tip or, with a rubber spatula, spread it on in decorative swirls. Scatter the shaved chocolate over the top of the pie and serve.

Pecan Pie

To make one 9-inch pie

1¼ cups all-purpose flour
4 tablespoons chilled vegetable shortening or lard
2 tablespoons chilled butter, cut in ¼-inch pieces
⅛ teaspoon salt
3 tablespoons ice water

Preheat the oven to 400°. In a large mixing bowl, combine the flour, vegetable shortening or lard, butter and salt. Use your fingertips to rub the flour and fat together until they look like flakes of coarse meal. Pour the ice water over the mixture, toss together, and press and knead gently with your hands only until the dough can be gathered into a compact ball. Dust very lightly with flour, wrap in wax paper and chill for at least ½ hour. Lightly butter a 9-inch pie plate. On a floured surface, roll the dough out into a circle about ⅛ inch thick and 13 to 14 inches in diameter. Lift it up on the rolling pin and unroll it over the pie plate, leaving enough slack in the middle of the pastry to enable you to line the plate without pulling or stretching the dough. Trim the excess pastry to within ½ inch of the rim of the pie plate and fold the extra ½ inch under to make a double thickness all around the rim. With the tines of a fork or with your fingers, press the pastry down around the rim.

To prevent the unfilled pastry from buckling as it bakes, either set another pie plate lightly buttered on the underside into the pastry shell or line it with a sheet of lightly buttered foil. In either case do not prick the pastry, or the filling will run out when it is added later. Bake the shell in the middle of the oven for 8 minutes, then remove the pan or foil and let the shell cool while you make the filling.

FILLING
4 eggs
2 cups dark corn syrup
2 tablespoons melted butter
1 teaspoon vanilla
1½ cups pecans

With a wire whisk or rotary beater, beat the eggs in a mixing bowl for about 30 seconds. Then slowly pour in the syrup and continue to beat until they are well combined. Beat in the melted butter and vanilla, and stir in the pecans. Carefully pour the filling into the pie shell. Bake in the middle of the oven for 35 to 40 minutes, or until the filling is firm. Serve the pie warm or cooled to room temperature.

Prune and Apricot Pie

To make one 9-inch pie

2½ cups all-purpose flour
8 tablespoons chilled vegetable shortening or lard
4 tablespoons chilled butter, cut into ¼-inch pieces
¼ teaspoon salt
6 tablespoons ice water

In a large mixing bowl, combine the flour, vegetable shortening or lard, butter and salt. Working quickly, use your fingertips to rub the flour and fat together until they look like flakes of coarse meal. Pour 6 tablespoons of ice water over the mixture, toss together, and press and knead gently with your hands until the dough can be gathered into a compact ball. Dust very lightly with flour, wrap in wax paper and chill for at least ½ hour.

Lightly butter a 9-inch pie plate and divide the ball of dough into 2 parts, one a third larger than the other. On a floured surface, roll out the larger half of dough into a circle about ⅛ inch thick and 13 to 14 inches in diameter. Lift it up on the rolling pin and unroll it over the pie plate. Be sure to leave enough slack in the middle of the pastry to enable you to line the plate without pulling or stretching the dough. Trim the excess pastry with a sharp knife, so that the pastry is even with the outer rim of the pie plate. Roll the smaller half of the dough into a rectangle 12 inches long and about ⅛ inch thick. With a sharp knife or pastry wheel, cut it into 6 strips about 1 inch wide. Refrigerate both the pie shell and the pastry strips while you make the filling.

FILLING
1½ cups dried pitted prunes
1½ cups dried apricots
1 cup shelled walnuts, coarsely chopped
½ cup sugar
1 teaspoon grated lemon rind
1 teaspoon vanilla
8 tablespoons (½ cup) melted butter, plus 1 tablespoon
1 cup heavy cream, whipped (optional)

Place the prunes and apricots in a small enameled or stainless-steel saucepan, and pour in enough water to cover them by about an inch. Bring the water to a boil. Boil rapidly for 4 to 5 minutes, then drain in a sieve. Dry the fruit with paper towels, and cut each prune and apricot into 4 pieces. Combine them in a mixing bowl with the walnuts, sugar, grated lemon rind and vanilla. Add the melted butter and, with a large spoon, mix together thoroughly. Spoon the filling into the pie shell. Arrange the reserved 3 strips of dough ¾ of an inch apart across the top of the pie and crisscross the other 3 strips of dough over them. With your fingers, tuck the ends firmly under the rim of the pie plate to secure them.

Preheat the oven to 350°. Brush the crisscross strips of pastry with the

1 tablespoon of melted butter and bake the pie in the middle of the oven for about 1 hour, or until the pastry is golden brown and the fruit is tender.

Serve warm or at room temperature, accompanied by unsweetened whipped cream if you like.

Key Lime Pie

To make one 9-inch pie

1 fully baked 9-inch pastry shell *(see banana cream pie, page 98)*
5 egg yolks
One 14-ounce can sweetened condensed milk
¾ cup fresh lime juice, preferably from Key limes
3 egg whites
1 cup heavy cream, whipped (optional)

Preheat the oven to 325°. With a wire whisk or rotary beater or electric mixer, beat the yolks of 5 eggs for 3 to 5 minutes until they are thick. Slowly beat in the condensed milk and then the lime juice. In another bowl, beat the egg whites until they form soft peaks and waver gently on the beater when it is lifted out of the bowl. Be careful not to overbeat; the whites should not be stiff. With a rubber spatula, fold them gently but thoroughly into the egg yolk mixture. Spoon the mixture at once into the cooled pie shell. Bake in the middle of the oven for 20 minutes, or until the filling is firm. Serve at room temperature or, as is often preferred, first chill the pie in the refrigerator. The whipped cream may be piped decoratively over the top of the pie or passed separately in a bowl.

NOTE: The tiny limes of the Florida Keys are seldom sold in stores. However, they are widely grown in the yards of Florida homes. Key limes are preferred for their flavor in this pie, but other limes may be used.

Baked Alaska

To serve 6 to 8

2 tablespoons soft butter
4 egg whites
Pinch of salt
1/4 cup sugar
4 egg yolks
1/2 teaspoon vanilla
1/2 cup all-purpose flour
1 cup orange marmalade or apricot preserves
1 to 2 tablespoons orange juice (optional)
1 quart vanilla ice cream, slightly softened

Brush a tablespoon of soft butter over the bottom and sides of an 11-by-16-inch jelly-roll pan. Line the pan with a 22-inch strip of wax paper and let the extra paper extend over the ends of the pan. Brush the remaining butter over the paper and scatter a small handful of flour over it. Tip the pan from side to side to spread the flour evenly. Then turn the pan over and rap it sharply to dislodge the excess flour.

Preheat the oven to 400°. In a mixing bowl, beat the egg whites and salt until they form soft, wavering peaks. Add the sugar, two tablespoons at a time, and beat until the whites cling to the beater solidly when it is lifted out of the bowl. In another small bowl, beat the egg yolks for about a minute, then add the vanilla. Mix a large tablespoon of the whites into the yolks, then pour the mixture over the remaining egg whites. Fold together, adding the 1/2 cup flour, two tablespoons at a time.

Pour the batter into the jelly-roll pan and spread it out evenly. Bake in the middle of the oven for about 12 minutes, or until the cake draws slightly away from the sides of the pan, and a small knife inserted in its center comes out dry and clean. Turn the cake out on a sheet of wax paper, then gently peel off the top layer of paper. Let the cake cool and cut it in half crosswise. Spread one layer with the cup of marmalade or apricot preserves (if it is too thick to spread, thin it by beating into it 1 or 2 tablespoons of orange juice) and place the second layer on top. Mold the softened ice cream on a sheet of aluminum foil into a brick the length and width of the cake. Wrap in the foil and freeze until solid.

THE MERINGUE
8 egg whites at room temperature
Pinch of salt
3/4 cup superfine sugar

About 10 minutes before serving, make the meringue. First, preheat the broiler to its highest point. Then, beat the egg whites and salt until they form soft peaks. Still beating, slowly pour in the sugar, and continue to beat for about 5 minutes, or until the egg whites are stiff and glossy. Remove the ice cream from the freezer and place it on top of the cake on a flat, ovenproof baking dish. Mask the cake and ice cream on all sides with the meringue, shaping the top as decoratively as you like. Slide the cake under the broiler for 2 to 3 minutes, and watch it carefully; it burns easily. The meringue should turn a pale, golden brown in 2 to 3 minutes. Serve at once before the ice cream begins to melt.

Pineapple Roll

To serve 6 to 8

One recipe of the cake for baked Alaska *(opposite)*
1½ cups chilled, heavy cream
4 tablespoons granulated sugar
1½ cups thoroughly drained, canned, crushed pineapple (1-pound, 4½-ounce can)
3 tablespoons confectioners' sugar

Make the cake as described on page 104 and turn it out on a double thickness of wax paper about 22 inches long. Remove the wax-paper lining from the top of the cake and let the cake cool to room temperature before filling and rolling it.

For the filling, beat the chilled cream with a large whisk or rotary or electric beater until it thickens lightly, then pour in the sugar and continue to beat until the cream is stiff enough to form firm peaks on the beater when it is lifted out of the bowl. With a rubber spatula, fold into it the thoroughly drained pineapple, and spread the mixture out evenly on top of the cake. Roll it up like a jelly roll and either serve at once or refrigerate, covered with a sheet of foil. Just before serving, sprinkle the exposed surface of the roll with the confectioners' sugar.

Lemon-Orange Ice

To make 1½ pints

¾ pound large sugar cubes
3 medium navel oranges
2 cups water
¼ cup fresh lemon juice
Small bunch fresh mint

Rub about 10 sugar cubes over the skins of the whole oranges to saturate them with the orange oil. Then squeeze the oranges. If they do not produce 1 cup of juice, use another orange. In a 1½ or 2-quart saucepan, bring the water and all of the sugar cubes to a boil over high heat, stirring until the sugar dissolves. Timing from the moment when it begins to boil, let the mixture boil briskly, without stirring, for 5 minutes. Immediately remove the pan from the heat and cool the syrup to room temperature. Stir in the orange juice and lemon juice, and pour into 2 ice-cube trays. Freeze for 3 to 4 hours at least, beating the ice after a half hour to break up the solid particles that will form on the bottom and sides of the tray. Continue to beat every half hour until the ice has a fine and snowy texture. Serve on chilled dessert plates or in sherbet glasses and garnish with the mint.

Old-fashioned Vanilla Ice Cream

To make about 1½ quarts

4 cups heavy cream
¾ cup sugar
⅛ teaspoon salt
1½-inch piece of vanilla bean

In a heavy 1½- or 2-quart enameled or stainless-steel saucepan, heat 1 cup of the cream, the sugar, salt and the vanilla bean over low heat, stirring until the sugar is dissolved and the mixture is hot but has not come to a boil. Remove from heat and lift out the vanilla bean. Split the bean in half lengthwise and, with the tip of a small knife, scrape the seeds into the cream mixture. When the mixture has cooled somewhat, stir in the remaining 3 cups of cream.

Pack a 2-quart ice-cream freezer with layers of finely crushed or cracked ice and coarse rock salt in the proportions recommended by the freezer manufacturer, adding cold water if the directions call for it. Then pour or ladle the cream mixture into the ice-cream container and cover it. Let it stand for 3 or 4 minutes. Then turn the handle, starting slowly at first, and crank continuously until the handle can barely be moved. Wipe the lid carefully, remove it and lift out the dasher. Scrape the ice cream off the dasher into the container and pack down with a spoon. Cover the container securely. Drain off any water in the bucket and repack it with ice and salt. Replace the container and let it stand 2 or 3 hours before serving.

Maple Mousse

To serve 6 to 8

1 envelope plus 2 teaspoons unflavored gelatin
½ cup cold water
1 cup pure maple syrup
4 egg yolks
½ cup brown sugar
4 egg whites
2 cups chilled heavy cream

Sprinkle the gelatin into the ½ cup of cold water and let it soften for about 5 minutes, then set the cup in a shallow pan of simmering water, and stir until the gelatin has dissolved and is clear. Combine with the maple syrup. In a large mixing bowl, beat the egg yolks with a whisk or a rotary or electric beater for 2 or 3 minutes until thick and lemon yellow. Beat into the yolks the maple syrup mixture and pour it into a small saucepan. Cook over moderate heat, stirring constantly, until the mixture thickens enough to coat the spoon heavily. Do not let it boil or the eggs will curdle. Remove from the heat, stir in the brown sugar and mix thoroughly. Transfer to a large bowl and cool to room temperature.

Meanwhile, beat the egg whites until they form unwavering peaks on the beater. In another bowl, whip the chilled cream until it holds its shape softly. With a rubber spatula, fold the cream gently but thoroughly into the maple syrup mixture, then fold in the egg whites, folding until streaks of white no longer show. Rinse a 1½-quart mold, preferably a charlotte mold, in cold water. Shake out the excess water and pour in the mousse mixture. Chill in the refrigerator for at least 4 hours, or until firm.

To unmold, run a knife around the inside edge of the mold, dip the bottom briefly in hot water and wipe it dry. Place a chilled platter on top of the mold, invert and rap it on the table. Chill until ready to serve.

Frozen Cranberry Mousse

To make about 2 quarts

8 egg yolks
1 cup bottled cranberry juice, or juice from drained cranberries plus enough bottled juice to make 1 cup
Two 16-ounce cans whole cranberries (about 4 cups), drained, or 4 cups freshly cooked cranberries, cooled and drained
1 tablespoon grenadine
4 egg whites
½ cup sugar
1 cup heavy cream, chilled

Beat the egg yolks with a whisk or a rotary or electric beater until they are thick and lemon yellow, then beat in the cranberry juice. Transfer the mixture to a small saucepan and cook over moderate heat, stirring constantly until it thickens enough to coat the spoon heavily. Under no circumstances allow this to boil or the eggs will curdle. Stir in the cranberries and grenadine, and pour into a bowl. Chill in the refrigerator for about ½ hour until it thickens slightly.

Beat the egg whites until they foam, then gradually beat in the sugar. Continue to beat until the whites form unwavering peaks on the beater when it is lifted out of the bowl. In another bowl whip the chilled cream until it holds its shape softly. With a rubber spatula, fold the cream gently but thoroughly into the thickened cranberry mixture, then fold in the egg whites, folding until streaks of white no longer show. Pour into refrigerator trays, or a 2-quart decorative mold or soufflé dish. Cover with foil and freeze until firm. The cranberry mousse may be served in scoops like ice cream, unmolded on a plate, or served directly from a soufflé dish.

Cold Orange Soufflé

To serve 6

2 envelopes unflavored gelatin
1 cup cold water
8 egg yolks
Two 6-ounce cans frozen orange juice concentrate, thoroughly defrosted but with no water added
8 egg whites
1 cup sugar
1 cup heavy cream, chilled
3 tablespoons sugar
½ cup heavy cream, whipped

Sprinkle the gelatin into the cup of cold water and let it soften for about 5 minutes. Meanwhile, with a whisk or a rotary or electric beater, beat the egg yolks until they are thick and lemon yellow. Beat in the softened gelatin.

Then cook the mixture in a small enameled or stainless-steel saucepan over moderate heat, stirring constantly, until it thickens enough to coat a spoon lightly. Do not let it come near a boil or it will curdle. Remove the pan from the heat and quickly stir in the defrosted orange juice. Transfer the mixture to a large mixing bowl and chill in the refrigerator for about ½ hour, or until it thickens to a syrupy consistency.

Beat the egg whites until they begin to froth, then pour in the sugar slowly and beat until the whites form unwavering peaks on the beater when it is lifted out of the bowl. In another bowl, whip the chilled cream until it holds its shape softly, then beat into it the 3 tablespoons of sugar. With a rubber spatula, fold the cream gently but thoroughly into the orange mixture (if it has set too firmly and formed lumps, beat gently with a whisk or rotary beater until smooth), then fold in the egg whites, folding until no streaks of white show. Tie a wax-paper collar around a 1½-quart soufflé dish. It should rise about 2 inches above the rim of the dish. Pour in the soufflé mixture up to the top of the collar, smooth the top with a spatula and chill in the refrigerator for at least 4 hours, or until firm. Carefully remove the collar and pipe decorative swirls or rosettes of whipped cream through a pastry bag on top of the soufflé.

Nesselrode Pudding

To serve 6

½ cup currants
¼ cup raisins
½ cup dark rum
4 egg yolks
1 cup sugar
3 cups heavy cream
An 8¾-ounce can unsweetened chestnut purée
1 teaspoon vanilla
1 teaspoon vegetable oil

Soak the currants and raisins in the rum for at least 15 minutes, then drain and reserve the rum and the fruit separately. Beat the egg yolks with a whisk or a rotary or electric beater for about a minute, then beat in all but 3 tablespoons of the cup of sugar. Continue to beat until the yolks are thick and fall slowly back into the bowl in a ribbon when the beater is lifted up. Heat 2 cups of the cream in a small saucepan until small bubbles begin to form around the edge of the pan. Slowly beat the hot cream into the egg yolk mixture, then return to the pan. Cook over moderate heat, stirring constantly, until the mixture thickens enough to coat a spoon lightly. Do not let the mixture come near a boil or it will curdle. Remove from the heat and stir in the chestnut purée, rum, vanilla, currants and raisins. Chill for about ½ hour.

Whip the remaining cup of chilled cream until it thickens slightly, then add the reserved 3 tablespoons of sugar and whip until the cream forms firm peaks on the beater when it is lifted out of the bowl. Fold it into the Nesselrode mixture with a rubber spatula, making sure the two are well combined. Brush a 1½-quart mold, preferably a charlotte mold, with the teaspoon of oil. Invert to drain any excess oil, then fill the mold with the Nesselrode mixture. Cover the top of the mold securely with foil and freeze the pudding for at least 6 hours until firm.

To unmold, run a knife around the inside edge of the mold, dip the bottom briefly in hot water and wipe it dry. Place a chilled serving platter on top of the mold, invert and rap it once on the table to dislodge it.

GARNISH

½ cup heavy cream whipped with 1 tablespoon confectioners' sugar
Candied chestnuts

Fit a pastry bag with a small star tip, fill the bag with the whipped cream, and pipe rosettes on the top and a decorative border around the bottom of the pudding. Place a small candied chestnut on each rosette.

Oatmeal Cookies

To make 24 cookies

1 cup all-purpose flour
½ teaspoon baking powder
½ teaspoon salt
8 tablespoons (1 quarter-pound stick) unsalted butter, softened
¾ cup dark brown sugar
¼ cup granulated sugar
1 egg
1 teaspoon vanilla
1 tablespoon milk
1¼ cups uncooked oatmeal

Preheat the oven to 350° and lightly butter two 11-by-17-inch baking sheets. Sift the flour, baking powder and salt together into a mixing bowl. Cream the butter, the brown sugar and the granulated sugar together by mashing them against the side of another mixing bowl with a wooden spoon. Stir in the egg, the vanilla extract and the milk, continuing to stir until the mixture is smooth. Beat in the flour mixture, a little at a time, then add the oatmeal, stirring until the mixture is well blended. Drop the batter by the tablespoonful onto the baking sheets, leaving space between for the cookies to expand. Bake for 12 minutes, or until the cookies are lightly browned on top.

Toll-House Cookies

To make 24 cookies

8 tablespoons (1 quarter-pound stick) softened butter
6 tablespoons granulated sugar
6 tablespoons dark brown sugar
½ teaspoon salt
½ teaspoon vanilla
¼ teaspoon cold water
1 egg
½ teaspoon baking soda
1 cup all-purpose flour
1 six ounce package semisweet chocolate bits
¾ cup coarsely chopped pecans
1 tablespoon soft butter

Preheat the oven to 375°. In a large mixing bowl, combine the butter, white and brown sugar, salt, vanilla and water, and beat them together with a large spoon until the mixture is light and fluffy. Beat in the egg and baking soda and when they are well combined add the flour, beating it in ¼ cup at a time. Then, gently but thoroughly fold in the chocolate bits and nuts.

With a pastry brush coat a cookie sheet evenly with the tablespoon of soft butter. Drop the cookie batter onto the sheet a tablespoon at a time, leaving about 1½ inches between the cookies. Gently pat down the tops of each cookie with a spatula, but don't flatten them entirely. Bake in the middle of the oven for about 12 minutes, or until the cookies are firm to the touch and lightly brown. Cool on a cake rack.

Butterscotch Brownies

To make 16 brownies

4 tablespoons butter
1 cup dark brown sugar
1 egg
1 teaspoon vanilla
½ cup all-purpose flour
1 teaspoon baking powder
½ teaspoon salt
½ cup coarsely chopped walnuts

Preheat the oven to 350°. Line an 8-inch-square baking pan with lightly buttered wax paper. Over low heat, melt the 4 tablespoons of butter in a small saucepan and add the brown sugar. Stir constantly until the sugar dissolves, then pour the mixture into a medium-sized mixing bowl. Cool until tepid. Beat in the egg and vanilla, and when they are thoroughly incorporated beat in the flour, baking powder and salt, first sifted together. Gently fold in the chopped walnuts and pour the batter into the baking pan. Bake in the center of the oven for about 25 minutes until the cake is firm to the touch and a small knife inserted in the center comes out clean. Let the cake cool for about 10 minutes, then cut it into 2-inch squares.

Chocolate Brownies

To make 16 brownies

2 squares unsweetened chocolate
½ cup butter
1 cup sugar
2 eggs
½ cup all-purpose flour
½ teaspoon baking powder
½ teaspoon salt
1 teaspoon vanilla
1 cup coarsely chopped walnuts

Preheat the oven to 350°. Melt the chocolate in a small heavy saucepan over low heat, stirring constantly, but do not let it come to a boil. Set it aside to cool slightly. Meanwhile, in a mixing bowl cream the butter and sugar together by beating them with a large spoon until the mixture is light and fluffy. Beat in the eggs, one at a time, and then the cooled chocolate. Sift the flour, baking powder and salt together into the mixture, and beat for 10 or 15 seconds, or until the ingredients are well combined. Stir in the vanilla and walnuts. Lightly butter an 8-inch-square baking pan. Pour in the batter and bake the brownies in the center of the oven for 30 to 35 minutes, or until a small knife inserted in the center comes out clean. Cool for about 10 minutes, then cut into 2-inch squares.

Recipe Index

Soups

Fruits and Vegetables

Meat

Poultry

Fish and Shellfish

Eggs and Cheese

Breads, Rolls and Breakfast Cakes

Desserts

Notes

Illustrations by Matt Greene.